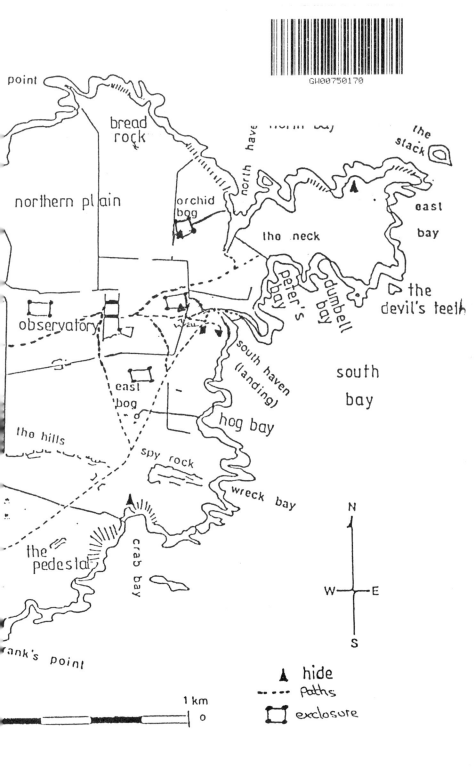

point

bread
rock

northern plain

the
stack

north haven

north bay

orchid
bog

the neck

east
bay

peter's
bay

dumbell
bay

the
devil's teeth

observatory

south haven
(landing)

south
bay

east
bog

hog bay

the hills

spy rock

wreck bay

the
pedestal

crab bay

ank's point

N

W — E

S

1 km

0

▲ hide

- - - - paths

⬚ exclosure

GW00750170

ABOVE: Ray Saunders, Author, Maurice Morgan –
sketched by Sam Robins. BELOW: Plaque at the
entrance to the cottage.

SKOKHOLM
The Islanders

BY

JOHN LEWIS

John Lewis

BARON
MCMXMCVII

PUBLISHED BY BARON BIRCH FOR QUOTES LIMITED
AND PRODUCED BY KEY COMPOSITION,
SOUTH MIDLANDS LITHOPLATES, CHENEY & SONS,
HILLMAN PRINTERS (FROME) LTD &
WBC BOOK MANUFACTURERS

© John Lewis 1997

ISBN 0 86023 586 6

Front cover prints

Copies of the cover design, presented as a mounted, limited edition
print, in black and white, are available from the artist – Peter
Partington, The Hall, Kettlebaston, IP7 7QA – price £10.00 carriage
inclusive.

CONTENTS

ACKNOWLEDGEMENTS

This book is based on my own diaries, kept during numerous visits to Skokholm and the Chatty Logs, to which visitors are invited to contribute.

I would especially like to thank Ronald Lockley, Anne Mark, Graham Gynn, Jean Lawman and Peter Sutcliffe for their contributions, Rod Billen for his excellent poems, Huw Morgan, Sam Robins and Helen Lewis for their sketches, Graham Thompson, Theresa Purcell, *South West News* for permission to use their photographs, and Stephen Sutcliffe for his comments on the first draft.

I have made every effort to trace contributors to the Logs; to any whom I have missed or failed to trace I apologise.

I would also like to pay tribute to the late David Stanbury, who died while the book was being written. His encouragement, friendship and enthusiasm were a tonic to all who knew him.

Skokholm is administered by The Wildlife Trust (West Wales), 7 Market Street, Haverfordwest, Pembrokeshire. Especial mention must be made of the island booking officer June Glennerster, who has put up with my impatient demands to be got to the island, often at very short notice; also Ken, Carl, Gary and Peter, who crew the *Dale Princess* and got me there.

I am also indebted to Peter Partington for the picture on the front cover.

Dedication

To Freddy, Poppy and John-John

FOREWORD by Steve Sutcliffe

I first met John Lewis on the boat to Skokholm in September 1981 when he was a visitor in need of a rest and I was leading a motley gang of enthusiastic and dedicated goat catchers. Our mission was to remove a herd of feral goats from the island. Like all such 'carefully planned' events, the learning curve was steep. It was not long before we found out that John was a farmer with some knowledge of goats and, although we initially ignored his 'that won't work' interjections, he was soon co-opted into the gang as chief goat catching advisor.

That was the start of John's unfailing and enthusiastic involvement in 'The Friends'; in particular, he generated the idea of work parties to carry out early season tasks on Skokholm. This both helped the wardens and improved the general state of the infrastructure of the island which had reached a fairly dilapidated state. The first job, in 1983, was re-roofing the Wheelhouse. Every year since then John has returned, sometimes several times, with his band of workers and a vast amount has been carried out – the value must be heading for the £100,000 mark; it is a massive effort.

He writes in this book of events on the island which would not otherwise be described and adds another perspective to the long, written history of Skokholm in an easily read package. To those who know the events, they are many, nice reminders of people and things which happened and they tell a little of island life in the 1980s and '90s – with a few historical bits thrown in for good measure.

If only we all kept diaries, took photos of ordinary things and told the tales as we see them – the world would be a better place.

ABOVE: The *Dale Princess* coming into South Haven and BELOW: the first view of the buildings from South Haven.

ISLAND OF DREAMS

The early morning sun sparkled on the rippling water and the sandstone cliffs had a welcoming glow as the boat, engine burbling as the exhaust dipped the waves, approached South Haven on the island of Skokholm. We passed a raft of puffins bobbing in the wavelets, guillemots and razorbills flew back and forth and cormorants on an offshore rock spread their wings to dry. The boat nosed its way towards the landing place and a grey seal slid off the rocks into the water.

When the boat came alongside the little quay I eagerly leapt ashore. I had arrived, I had achieved a long-held ambition to visit the dream island made famous by the writings of R. M. Lockley. I was met by Graham, the resident warden who, with his keen eyes trained to notice the arrived of unusual bird species, flowing locks and straggly beard, had the look of an Old Testament prophet.

Together we walked up the steep track from the landing place. A low wall on the left prevented the island dumper truck, the only vehicle on the island, from toppling over into the shallow valley below and a bank to the right was covered in thrift and campion. Half way up the track was an old limekiln, its top overgrown with brambles in which was a spotted flycatcher. Puffins on the far bank stood like little aldermen outside their burrows and oystercatchers 'pip-pipped' as they fluttered around.

At the top of the track vast banks of bluebells and bracken came into view, alive with the buzz of insects in the summer sun. Beyond the bluebells was a meadow, close cropped by rabbits and a small flock of goats, which over the years had been allowed to run wild over the island.

On the far side of the meadow were the buildings – an odd shaped cottage, what looked like an old barn and some rough shacks. These I discovered later comprised the Warden's quarters, visitors' rooms and a kitchen-cum-dining room.

The tang of the salt air mixed with the smell of the bracken gave me a surge of adrenalin. I wanted to run out and grasp the whole island; run right round it, climb to its highest point, penetrate the depths of its caves and see all the birds that had ever been recorded since it was set up as a bird observatory in 1933. I only had a day and there was so much to see.

The top of Skokholm is a more or less level plateau with rock outcrops and low hillocks. It was the highest of these, the aptly named Spy Rock that I decided would be the first place to visit. This would give an idea of the layout and extent of this two hundred and forty acre island.

After a short climb I reached the top and in so doing aroused a colony of lesser black back gulls, who swooped and dived noisily around, resenting my intrusion.

From the top I could easily see the extent of the island. A track at the foot of Spy Rock led from the harbour, through a cutting in some low hills, to a white-painted lighthouse at the westernmost tip. Between was a low boggy area with open spaces of water; looking through my binoculars I spotted a brood of mallard.

Further round was a larger pond on which a flock of gulls were splashing around washing the salt from their wings. To the north a flat plain, on which lapwings and oystercatchers were nesting, stretched to the northernmost point of the island.

In the middle distance were the cottage and buildings nestling under the shelter of a low mound. To the north east was a smaller area of land of around thirty acres, forming a promontory known as The Neck.

Way out to the west I could see the island of Grassholm where there is a rapidly expanding gannetry. It was a clear day and, looking through my binoculars, I could see the gannets swirling around over the island. Even further west I could see The Smalls lighthouse, and to the north west there was Ramsey Island and the South Bishop Light.

Skomer Island filled the view to the north and Skomer Head reminded me of the shape of a sperm whale floating on the water. Middleholm between Skomer and the mainland concentrated the tidal flow to form the notorious Jack Sound, a treacherous tide rip, always to be treated with the greatest respect.

Two miles to the east were the mainland, St Anne's Head and the entrance to Milford Haven. A large oil tanker was slowly nosing its way into port and the Irish sail training ship *Asgard*, sails fully set and scarcely drawing, was making slow progress towards her home port.

I came down from Spy Rock and lingered awhile watching the large colony of puffins in the bay below. They were flying round it, then far to sea and back again, very often with beaks full of sand eels. After a few circuits they would come in to land beside their burrows, wait awhile, then either enter the burrow or take another flight.

I decided to make for the lighthouse and wandered along the track, marvelling at the large number of lesser black back gulls nesting all over the island. There were gulls every few yards, and they demonstrably resented my intrusion if I wandered from the path into their colony.

10

The mallard in the boggy pond had disappeared into the rushes but, in a more open pond to the left of the track, I saw two ringed plover and a dunlin. My list of bird sightings was increasing by leaps and bounds.

It was midday when I reached the lighthouse and I thought I would rest awhile on the rocks and eat my sandwiches while looking at the sea. I had not been there long before a school of porpoises, at least six of them, disported themselves just offshore. Shag, scoter and gannets were passing all the time. The gannets were a delight especially as, circling over the water, they would suddenly fold their wings and javelin-like, dive into the waves. A few second later they would emerge with mackerel in their beaks, which they would swallow whole then, splashing wings flapping, take off again.

Moving away from the lighthouse towards the north along the west side of the island, I passed through an area honeycombed by manx shearwater burrows. I had to take great care where I put my feet, otherwise I would crash through the roof of a burrow and expose the bird inside to the predation of the gulls.

Some thirty five thousand of these birds nest on the island and, even though I took great care, I still broke through a couple of burrows. Having carefully cleared away the dirt, I covered the hole with a large stone, so the gulls could not take the bird inside in this, the nesting season. Evidence of gull predation is to be found all too often in the number of shearwater corpses lying around.

Although they are amazing fliers, feeding far out to sea and wintering in the south Atlantic, they are vulnerable when they come into land. Their feet and legs seem to be placed in the wrong position on their bodies, so that they are front heavy. This means they can only shuffle slowly along and, unless they quickly find their burrow, they are easy prey.

The shearwater burrows are all up the west side of the island, as are colonies of guillemots on the cliff ledges and razorbills and fulmars on individual nest sites on the rocks.

Looking from the lighthouse towards Hard Point I had a splendid view of the Mad Bay coastline, with headlands and inlets carved out of the red sandstone by the full force of Atlantic Westerlies over many centuries.

On the cliff tops and running back inland were huge beds of sea pink, campion and goldenrod. The effect was magical and my camera shutter was clicking from every fresh angle.

A sudden uproar and whirling around of the gulls made me look up to seek the cause of the disturbance – a buzzard, lazily soaring overhead.

After a quick look at Hard Point to see a club of guillemots at water's edge and fulmars gliding around in the updrafts, with time pressing I wanted to get round The Neck.

Passing through colonies of puffins standing guard over their burrows, I eventually came to The Stack, an isolated islet at the eastern end of the island. Here I could hear the roar of the tide rip through Broad Sound and the sea gushing like a rapidly flowing river through the narrow strip of water that separated The Stack from The Neck. A cairn of stones on the top showed me that someone had got over and at that moment I vowed I would return to Skokholm one day and add to that pile.

Continuing round The Neck I came to an outcrop of rocks known as The Devil's Teeth and was rewarded by a group of purple sandpipers and, a little further on at the water's edge, a flock of turnstones.

I made my way back to the buildings, where the Wardens were preparing the evening meal. I chatted to them for a while and they gave me a cup of tea. How I envied them their simple life, without telephone, television, motor car and all the trappings with which we have surrounded ourselves and mistakenly believe to be so essential.

The sun was setting in the western sky, the boat was due and I had to leave. A flight of curlew came in from the mainland to roost for the night and I heard the plaintive call of a whimbrel. As we sailed away, Skokholm slowly became enveloped in a sea mist and only the deep note of the foghorn from the lighthouse told me that I had not been dreaming.

I vowed to return at the earliest possible opportunity, little realising that I was about to begin an interesting and exciting new chapter in my life.

> The glory of the sunset and the rainbow's double arc,
> Spread across the heavens as the light was growing dark.
> There was silence all around, save the cries of many birds,
> Eternal living witnesses of wonders without words.

Poem by Anne Reed, 28 August 1954

ABOVE: A group of puffins forms a Welcoming Committee. BELOW: View from Spy Rock – the road through The Cutting to the lighthouse; South Bog is in the middle distance.

13

ABOVE: The buildings before re-construction by the Work Parties. BELOW: South Haven and The Neck.

GET BILLY

The first visit took place in the early summer of 1981 and I could not wait to get back to spend a week exploring this unique sanctuary. The summer on the farm that year was an exceptionally busy one and it was not until the last week in September that I felt able to take time off. I acccordingly rang Mrs Eileen Williams, the island booking officer for the West Wales Naturalists' Trust. In accepting my booking she casually mentioned that I would be going over in the company of a Trust party, who were going to round up and evacuate the islands' herd of feral goats.

As instructed I presented myself at 10 am at Dale Sailing Company and, to my consternation, found I was going over in the company of a rough and rowdy group of eight goat catchers. I was feeling pretty run down with one thing and another and saw my chances of a quiet peaceful week going for a Burton, especially as it was made abundantly clear that, visitor though I may be, I would be expected to pull my weight in the goat catch and no slacking would be tolerated. I nearly expired on the spot!

I also met the boatman-cum-proprietor of Dale Sailing Company, Campbell Reynolds, who would be taking us over in the *Dale Princess*. Campbell to everybody, he was one of those rare characters to whom you immediately warm and feel you have made a friend. Full of fun, kindliness, completely unflappable in a crisis, he commanded affection and esteem from everyone with whom he came in contact.

At that time the island boat service went from the little village of Dale in the Milford Haven estuary. Because it was only possible to load directly into the boat at about half tide, transfers from boat to shore were either made by inflatable dinghy or an ex-army DUKW, an amphibious vehicle equally at home on land or water. Because there was a fair amount of stuff to go over the transfer was made by the DUKW to the *Dale Princess*, lying at anchor offshore.

The waters of Milford Haven are sheltered but, as we rounded St Anne's Head, we met the Atlantic swell and the sea became quite bumpy. By this time I had got to know the goat catchers a bit better and concluded that one or two might be quite tolerable – in small doses!

Because of the state of the sea and of the tide the *Princess* could not get into the diminutive harbour and we and our gear had to be ferried across in the inflatable dinghy, which had to make several trips.

15

We were met by the island Wardens, Graham and Liz Gynn, the previous week's visitors and last but by no means least the figurehead of the *Alice Williams*. Wrecked on the island in 1928, and salvaged by Ronald Lockley, the figurehead was set up on the clifftop and in those days used to look out over the harbour.

More recently it was discovered that exposure to the weather was not doing her any good. What was more, she was unique and intrinsically valuable, so she is now housed in the farm buildings.

Having safely landed and with the previous week's visitors having departed, we made our way to the buildings, where we were allotted our rooms by Liz.

I was given the one called 'The Gunners' in the cottage. All the rooms carry a name of nautical origin. So we have Port, Starboard, Carpenter's, Steward's, Bosun and the Angel Loft.

David Stanbury, whose sudden death, besides being a great loss to the island, cut short the research he was doing into the island's early history, recorded that 'the dwelling house was built after a whimsical manner with suitable farm offices, by Captain David Allen, Gentleman', between 1766 and 1776. It is almost certainly on the site of the ferreter's store house repaired in 1387, which in turn was probably built on the prehistoric hut circle that went with the ruined walled enclosure on the knoll behind.

In the course of one of the last conversations I had with David, he informed me that, having consulted the Army list of the time, he had discovered that Captain Allen had fought alongside General Wolfe, when he took Quebec from the French in 1759.

On entering the houses you find yourself in a large lobby with rough flagged floor. From this a door leads off into The Ringing Room, now a bedroom but, as its name suggests, it was once the place where trapped birds were brought to be ringed and recorded before being released.

Other doors lead to a toilet and a comfortable Common Room, which houses a modest but well-equipped library. Its content largely consists of natural history and bird reference books, although there are several volumes of fiction by popular authors. The Common Room is where everyone meets for coffee after the evening meal to assist the Warden make up the daily log of birds, insects and sea mammal sightings.

We had no sooner unpacked than a ship's bell was rung by Graham to summon us to lunch. All meals are served in the old farm barn, called The Wheelhouse, which has been converted into a kitchen-dining room.

A long table was set down the middle and benches placed on either side. Graham, as Warden in charge, sat at the head of the table with the brass bound wheel of the *Alice Williams* hung up on the chimney breast behind him. Even though it was almost fifty years since she was wrecked, there was and is still ample evidence of her presence. Most of the rafters and timbers in the cottage and the stairs to The Angel Loft were taken from her, as were many other features in the farmyard and outbuildings.

Named after the principal owner's wife, she was an undistinguished representative of a fleet of sailing coasters common in the nineteenth and early twentieth century. She was of 137 tons, 80 ft long, 20 ft 5 inches beam and her hold was twelve feet deep. Her carrying capacity was around 220 tons and her cargoes were mainly coal, pig iron, timber, china clay and grain.

She was somewhat out of the ordinary in that she carried a figurehead, unusual in a ship of that date and size. One other figurehead survives from a boat named *Mary Welch*, which was built in the same yard as *Alice Williams* at Llanelli. This also represented the wife of her owner and it is likely it was carved by the same person.

She sailed from Llanelli to Falmouth on her maiden voyage on 3 January 1885. Her master was John Meyrick, and also aboard were the mate, two able seamen and two apprentices. It would seem that at some stage she was altered and reclassified so as to be able to take part in the deep sea trade. In this capacity she carried cargoes to and from Marseilles, Stockholm, Riga and Bilbao in northern Spain.

Her career was not particularly remarkable or distinguished. But in February 1928 she was carrying a cargo of coal to the north west, encountered strong winds and became unmanageable off St Anne's Head. Her crew, thinking she was sinking, took to the boats.

But for the fact that she was wrecked on the doorstep of a talented author, who immortalised her in his writings, she would have been long forgotten.

Rod Billen, the island poet, has also recently immortalised her:

The Love of Alice

'By Blacksmith's landing I sat and watched
The sun drop into the sea,
When swift and low, as a bolt from a bow
The Raven came to me.

He perched nearby and stared at me,
Greeting me with a croak.
His eyes of coal peered into my soul
Until at last he spoke.

Alice Williams forgave you
And all your kind he cried.
On the night of the storm, when alone and forlorn
She rolled over and finally died.

In terrible seas and howling winds
A time for men to be brave,
But her mariners fled and left her for dead
And she slid to her watery grave.

Yet in the calm of the morning
High and dry on the rocks she lay,
Then men came with rules and with ropes and with tools
And they carried her treasures away.

She gave them her timbers and bulkheads
And her coals to keep them warm.
With her fittings and rails, her wheel and her sails
She helped them to rebuild their home.

At the final count-down, in the book of time,
Alice Williams will never know fame,
But let you who are able to eat from her table
Raise a glass to honour her name.

ALICE WILLIAMS.'

After lunch we were split up into groups for such tasks as washing-up, peeling potatoes and other similar chores. A rota system was worked out so that we did not have to do the same task on successive days, which at least lent some variety to the job in hand.

We were then taken on a tour of the island and shown the points of interest, how to use the bird observation hides and, most important, shown where not to go for fear of damaging the shearwater and puffin burrows. Finally we met the goats, thirteen of them led by an enormous billy with terrific horns. He really was a most handsome fellow.

There was much learned discussion, led by Stephen Sutcliffe, the chairman of the island management committee, as to how we should set about catching them. There was general agreement, with myself as the sole dissenting voice, that the best thing to do would be to drive them into some big nets we had brought, when it got dark, the theory presumably being that they would be fast asleep and would not see us coming. My comments, that they would be a good deal more wideawake, have better night vision and know their way around the island a good deal better than we who had just arrived, were ignored.

We had dinner early that first night and set out under a full moon. Those of us who did not know the island all that well made our way to Tabernacle Rock and settled down to wait while Bob Burgess and Stephen Sutcliffe hunted around in the gloaming, trying to located the missing herd.

After what seem an interminable wait in the cold, listening to the screech of shearwaters and the cheeping of storm petrels, the goats were located on a headland known as The Bluffs. Quickly the nets were erected in what were thought to be the goat 'flight paths', and a couple of beaters attempted to drive them into the trap. Not surprisingly it was quickly discovered that the goats had excellent night vision and used flight paths of which we were unaware.

This had all taken two and a half hours and spirits were decidedly flagging. We were inclined to give up for the night and try again in daylight, when there was less chance of someone falling over a cliff. There had already been one or two good tries, stumbling around in the dark. However, our spirits were revived by Bob's sudden appearance, full of determination and lighthouse keeper's booze.

There was a good moon, which was almost as good as daylight, and those of us whose sporting instincts had been aroused were inclined to give it another try. After a lot of casting around we at last managed to corner six of them on a cliff ledge at Dip Gully. To get there we had chased all over a shearwater colony which Graham had specifically asked us to avoid.

With some difficulty we slipped a running noose over their horns so that Alan Wynde, a vet attached to the party, could climb down and sedate them, the idea being that they, being on the wild side, would be generally easier to handle and their struggles would not take them and us over the cliff. Unfortunately he misjudged the dose; instead of quietening them down he put them right out. We then had the job of lugging their dead weight up the cliff in the dark.

The lighthouse keepers had a dump truck to cart their gear from the harbour and which we were allowed to use. We loaded the goats into this and carted them back to the buildings.

We had been so pre-occupied with catching the goats that no-one had given much thought about how we were to hold them once they had been caught. Various suggestions such as penning them up in the bunkhouse or the loo were abandoned, after Alan and I had insisted that this would be a sure way of inducing pneumonia, after their life in the open air. By this time I was being allowed a small measure of credence for my occasional comments.

19

We eventually settled on hobbling them and tying them up by the horns to some firm anchorage in the yard. It was useless to think of penning them up loose in the yard because, although the walls were good and sound, they could easily have climbed over the top.

By the time we had got everything fixed up it was two o'clock in the morning; after drams and coffee all round we eventually got to bed.

After breakfast the following morning we were keen to have another go at the goats. We soon discovered that those that were left, led by the big Billy, were thoroughly alarmed and quick off the mark. We discarded the nets and relied on our ability to run them down until they were tired and retreated to some cliff ledge or cave. We got two like this after they had led us a dance over the rocks in Wildgoose Bay. The remainder of the herd had apparently vanished so we returned to base for lunch.

After lunch and acting on a hunch we thought we would go and have a look in The Quarry, so called because of its quarry-like appearance and the possibility that stone was taken from there to build the lighthouse.

Sure enough four of them were holed up in a cave, we managed to grab three and Mick Brown was the hero of the day in reaching out and grabbing the Big Billy as he tried to shoot past. The fourth goat came at us up the ramp out of the quarry and jumped clean over our heads.

While all this goat chasing was going on we were expected to keep a good look out and a note of all the birds we saw during the day. It is a feature of Skokholm life that, after the evening meal, we gather in the common room and the warden records all the birds that have been sighted during the day, and enters them in the log. Being autumn there were of course no nesting birds but this is a good time of the year for migrants. We all hoped to be the first to spot say a black headed bunting, a lapland bunting or a scarlet rosefinch.

The evenings were chilly, so we got a good driftwood fire going and, what with the hiss of the Tilley lamps hanging from the ceiling, the conversation of a good crowd who between them have been to some pretty odd places, I would not have wanted to be anywhere else in the world. I had by this time revised my initial impressions of my companions. Many of them have since become lifelong, much valued friends.

Peter Sutcliffe was moved to express his sentiments in poetic vein and made the following entry in the logbook retained for visitors' comments.

20

'Like an army force across the plain,
They bore down on their prey.
Clear calls of command did fill the air
Like:- "Where'd they go, what yer say, which way".
Goats to the right of them, goats to the left of them
Finally caught and cornered and put to sleep.
Hunters and Quarry group together
In one large goat smelly heap.
Quickly counting the quarry
It's found that two are free,
A shout of command from Bob
Like "Leave the buggers to me".
September fourteenth, of nineteen eighty one
A sad and miserable day,
Two goats from Spy Rock
Watch their friends being taken away.'

In the end we accounted for those as well.

The next morning, a Monday, was wet and rough. Some of the dafter ones among us dressed up in waterproofs and went to look for the missing goats. I went out to Purple Cove, and had to really lean against wind and rain. I met Graham, who told me I was wasting my time, with which comment I was inclined to agree.

He walked on towards the lighthouse and I worked back to North Point. Suddenly a goat shot up the cliff face in front of me and made off towards the lighthouse. Graham saw him coming and headed him off to Tabernacle Rock. He went through South Bog and we last saw him dimly in the mist going through The Cutting towards Spy Rock. We hunted all round but could not find him, so back to the kitchen for coffee.

By this time the mist was thick and a heavy sea had got up. According to the schedule a Sea King helicopter on a training exercise should have arrived to evacuate the goats to the mainland and eventually to Cardigan Wildlife Park. Because of the atrocious weather the evacuation was put back for twenty-four hours.

The weather cleared a bit after tea and I went for a walk along the cliffs towards the lighthouse, then turned along the path to Mad Bay. I saw three or four people coming out of the mist in the distance, then all at once I saw a goat coming straight at me. I tried to head him off but he went off towards Franks Rocks. My nice quiet walk had turned into another goat chase. We lost him and started casting around when someone stepped on him in the bracken. He shot off towards the lighthouse and we lost him again.

Feeling sure he was somewhere in the quarry we hunted high and low, when suddenly I spotted some fresh tracks half way down, which suddenly petered out. Close by was a crack between two boulders and there he was. This left one goat which had completely disappeared. He never did turn up and I thought he went over a cliff on the first night, but a couple of years later his skeleton was found in a cleft in the quarry.

Spot on 2.15 pm the following afternoon a Sea King helicopter from RAF Brawdy touched down on the meadow in front of the buildings. Alan put the goats under heavy sedation, the smaller ones were put in the helicopter's cabin and the bigger ones, including Big Billy, were carried in a net slung beneath.

So they were whisked off to start a new life in Cardigan Wildlife Park. Soon afterwards the goat catchers left on the *Dale Princess* and the Wardens and myself were left in sole occupation. On the Friday the mainland and Skomer looked close, the sky became overcast and the sea was like molten lead. Wind, rain and high seas blew up and continued all day Saturday, making it impossible for the boat to come and fetch me off.

By Saturday night the rain had stopped and the sky had cleared. It was a brilliant moonlit night with clouds scudding across the face of the moon. I walked across to Mad Bay, where there was still a strong wind and a high sea running; it was exilherating. The spray from the breaking waves was carried right up to the cliff top, as wave after wave of unchecked Atlantic rollers crashed against the rocks at my feet. I stood watching for about half an hour, marvelling at the tremendous forces of the deep.

I walked round the island, alone in this mad wild landscape, lit by the unearthly light of the moon, deafened by the wind and the sound of waves breaking. Late-hatched shearwater chicks occasionally fluttered at my feet as they attempted to find a small hillock from which they could launch themselves into the unknown.

The red flashing light from the lighthouse added to the atmosphere of unreality. I felt that this was how it was at the beginning and how it must have felt to be one of the Lords of the dawn of Creation.

ABOVE: First view of South Haven. BELOW: The
late Campbell Reynolds in his usual friendly mood.

OPPOSITE: Unloading the boat. ABOVE: A dumper load of baggage reversing up the track from the harbour. BELOW: The cottage, 'a whimsical house'.

25

LEFT: The figurehead BELOW: of the *Alice Williams*. (Reproduced by permission of The National Maritime Museum) RIGHT: Theresa Purcell rings the bell for lunch.

ABOVE: Some of the goats, and BELOW: the last
one to be caught, from left to right : Peter Sutcliffe,
Mick Brown, Alan Wynde, Stephen Sutcliffe, John
Lambe and Graham Gynn.

27

LEFT: Emma Wynde with her pet goat. RIGHT: Guillemots on the ledges. BELOW: John Buxton and his wife Marjorie, née Lockley, looked after the island in 1939. (Reproduced by kind permission of the Editor of *This England*).

EARLY DAYS

I spent the following winter reading up and finding out all I could about the island. I learned that R. M. Lockley, at the age of twenty three, had in 1927 achieved the ambition that many of us yearn for and never realise. He had 'discovered' Skokholm, taken over the lease from one Bulldog Edwards, who in turn leased the island from the Dale Castle Estate.

He found the buildings in a dilapidated state and initially he and his companions lived in the barn. The cottage had a hole in the roof and was at that time uninhabitable.

Lockley had taken up residence in October and by a, for him, happy chance the topsail schooner *Alice Williams* was wrecked in the inlet now known as Wreck Cove, the following February. Acting quickly, he bought the wreck from the underwriters for five pounds. It was a Godsend for, from the timbers he was able to repair the cottage and outbuildings and her cargo of coal lasted for many years.

These and many other adventures are well chronicled in his books *Dream Island, Way to an Island* and others. After the first winter, when he had made the buildings reasonably habitable, he married, and brought his bride Doris to the island where eventually their daughter Anne was born.

They lived on the sale of rabbits, fishing, the produce of a few sheep, goats and two cows. He speaks of collecting 4,000 gulls' eggs over a six week period, the majority of which were pickled for future use. Their needs were simple and necessities, beyond what the island could supply, minimal.

A naturalist at heart, although he had taken the island ostensibly to farm, he quickly realised it was unique in the variety and quantity of its birdlife. Encouraged by the late Harry Witherby, who let him have a supply of rings, he began studies on bird migration, concentrating on the manx shearwater. The result quickly attracted attention and in July 1934 he and Skokholm were honoured to host the eighth International Ornithological Congress. Some measure of the importance of the occasion is indicated by the fact that two Royal Navy destroyers were seconded for the conveyance of the delegates.

Lockley's tenure of the island came to an abrupt halt in 1940. The war had taken a turn for the worse, France had fallen, invasion appeared imminent and officialdom declared the island must be evacuated. He obtained the tenure of the peninsula known as Dinas Island which he reclaimed and farmed. It was at this time that I learnt about him as a contributor to a publication called *The Farmer & Stockbreeder*. This published a number of articles in which he related his experiences at Dinas, where he established a reputation as an expert on growing flax.

Even though Skokholm had been placed out of bounds because of the war, he managed to cross over on a number of occasions and he was delighted to renew his acquaintance and maintain touch with a number of shearwaters he had ringed pre-war.

With the cessation of hostilities plans were made for re-opening the observatory. On 12 April 1946 the first landing was made to inspect the premises. Those in the party were recorded as R. M. Lockley, John Fursdon, P. Lockley and three others. The house and buildings were inspected. The house is recorded as being 'fair', but the yard buildings needed repairs.

An entry in the log states the party spent three hours on the island. They recorded a raven's nest on the east side, one fulmar in South Haven and that a peregrine flew from Mad Bay in the direction of Skomer, chased by lapwings of which there were several. In addition they saw twelve turnstones, puffins and razorbills on the water, a buzzard and a chaffinch in the garden, wheatears and one jackdaw.

They evidently decided the island was habitable because they took up residence the following day. The next few days were mainly spent repairing the house and buildings and setting up the bird traps, so that the ringing programme could commence.

John Fursdon was appointed Warden in an honorary capacity. He had had previous experience of Skokholm, having helped Lockley and the Baron transport sheep and ponies to Martinshaven when the island was evacuated in 1940. He tells of shortages of timber, wire netting, petrol and food, how they had to live off the land and how often the basic necessities had to be improved from what was to hand.

He speaks of the help he received in those early days from such people as Bill and Penny Condry, who took over the housekeeping. The supply officer at Martinshaven was ex-Wren Pat Higginson, who afterwards became Mrs Peter Conder. Then there was Reuben Codd, who would come to the rescue in his boat when the Dale Fort boat failed to arrive.

Of course there were the lighthouse keepers without whom they could not easily have managed. He tells of how, when the keepers wanted anything sent from home on the next boat, they would broadcast their wants on medium wave 191, which their wives would pick up on their ordinary radio sets at home.

Going back to the beginning, the parent body was the Pembrokeshire Bird Protection Society, which went through several name changes and is now known as The Wildlife Trust (West Wales).

In 1945, for it had lapsed during the war years, it was revived by R. M. Lockley, with the support of his brother-in-law, the soldier-poet John Buxton. John married Marjorie Lockley and they acted as caretakers on Skokholm in the summer of 1939 when, because of the war, Ronald had to evacuate to the mainland. In later years he became a language don and widely respected Emeritus Fellow of New College, Oxford.

Peter Conder and John Barret also gave their support. All three were brave men, having spent five long years as prisoners-of-war in Germany. To preserve their sanity they occupied their time in birdwatching, Buxton doing some useful work on redstarts, but his health had been permanently damaged as a result of his experiences.

Little thinking that he faced five long years of captivity, he wrote the following lines to his wife Marjorie from his prison camp in Germany. Those who know Skokholm will have little difficulty recognising the destination of his thoughts.

'I see before me England, whose am I
Living, and when I die.
My names are names she gave me at the font;
I speak the speech she taught me; and, by and by,
When I was far, England was all my want.

When I was far! who am a prisoner now
Save as my thoughts allow
Some liberty to dream of being free,
To dream I stand on England's rocky prow
Where it thrusts Westward through the cloven sea.

Oh! I can see you standing at my side
Watching the wild goose tide
As you so often stood a year ago,
My dear companion, my delightful bride,
To whom all joy and all my faith I owe...'

(Reproduced by kind permission of *This England* magazine.

Lockley had a forty-two year lease dating from 1927, which he handed over to what was then called the West Wales Field Society.

Natural History Study Centres were set up on both Skokholm and Skomer and administered from Lockley Lodge at Martinshaven. This became so successful that it was decided to move the centre to Dale Fort and John Fursdon was appointed as volunteer caretaker warden.

There was then an approach from the Council for Promotion of Field Studies, who offered to co-operate, running the Fort as one of their centres. This offer was accepted, provided the Society could retain an office in the Fort. John Barret was put forward for the job of Warden at the Fort and as such was responsible for administering Skokholm.

It was then that the Field Studies Council erected a hut in the courtyard, but this was contrary to the terms of the lease and had to be dismantled. This explains the concrete slab, which is still there.

John Fursdon was delighted when Ronald Lockley allowed the Baron, the late George Harris, to stay with him on Skokholm for that first season. This extraordinary character had been Lockley's companion, confidant and general factotum for many years. His stories and experiences, as related to Lockley, were published in a book entitled *A Pot of Smoke*, published by Harrap.

Running away from home at the age of thirteen he was adopted by a family with nine children and was put to work in a London factory. Bored to distraction he stuck it for two years and then, at fifteen, having been turned down as under age by the Army, he joined the Navy. He was shipwrecked off the coast of Mozambique on his first voyage. Having been shipwrecked he was entitled to be discharged and he joined the Royal Horse Artillery.

His first taste of action was in West Africa to remonstrate with natives who had been cooking missionaries. In his opinion the latter had cooked up trouble for themselves by trying to force the piccaninnies to wear trousers, against their natural inclination!

He saw service in South Africa, was wounded in the Boer War and sent to hospital. On being discharged he was grabbed by General Kitchener to help round up malingering officers in Cape Town. He then went to Bloemfontein and Kimberley and was captured by the Boers, whom he thought to be rather a good lot.

When his time in the Army was up he went to Canada where, after a brief spell in the motor trade, he took a quarter section of land (160 acres) in Alberta. He built up a useful timber business but, after getting badly frostbitten as the result of an accident, he was advised to leave Canada – otherwise the cold would get him.

After all these experiences, when they had to load ponies and the cow into an open boat he said that that was 'chicken feed' compared with loading lions and tigers in Africa. Setting up a workshop on Skokholm, he quickly set about licking the place into shape. He is mentioned in the log as having celebrated his 73rd birthday by climbing down to Crab Bay for driftwood. He is also mentioned as having splinted someone's leg after they had broken it during a nightjar drive.

The logs are mostly bare records of bird sightings, wind strengths, the weather and the comings and goings of visitors and helpers who arrived and departed on an irregular basis. Students paid 25 pence a day full board and others three guineas a week plus 25 pence boat fare.

They started off by living and cooking in the cottage, but soon moved the dining room and kitchen to the Wheelhouse, where they had a lot of trouble with the chimney smoking.

Trapping and ringing was the order of the day and they quickly got this organised, because it is recorded that on 30 April they ringed 54 whitethroats, six willow warblers and six sedge warblers. They would have done more but the supply of rings ran out.

On 25 June it was recorded that to date 1,305 birds had been ringed of which 888 were shearwaters. A number of female glowworms were brought over from Skomer and released in South Haven.

War debris drifted past The Stack in the shape of a mine. It became anchored half a mile east of Spy Rock. Attempts to explode it with a .22 rifle failed. Ten days later a boat came to inspect the mine and two days after that the tug *Empire Netta* came to destroy it but, although several rounds were fired and hits registered, the mine failed to explode. War must have made the authorities blasé about this sort of situation because another seven days went by before it was removed by 'early morning visitors', at 0800 hours.

There are frequent references to Caroline, a little Welsh black cow, who was brought to the island because John Fursdon could not tolerate goat's milk. On one occasion she got into the kitchen, with disastrous results! She was not always co-operative when it came to milking time and would run from The Neck to the lighthouse, thereby depleting her milk yield by several pints.

Other livestock recorded as being on the island included a flock of 'wild' Soay sheep, numbering thirty three including the lambs.

The year came to an end and the island was closed up for the winter on 2 October. The number of total ringings for the year is not recorded in the log but some idea might be extrapolated from the record of 26 July, for up to that date 2,398 had been ringed during the month.

One of the last things John Fursdon did was to negotiate with the Post Office to pay the West Wales Field Society three pounds a time for delivering the Skokholm mail. This meant that the cost of boat trips to the island was covered.

ABOVE: The South Bog lesser blackback gull
colony; BELOW: Northern Plain gull colony and
The Stack.

34

RINGING THE GULLS

Peter Conder was appointed Warden for 1947 and he remained in post for eight years. Other members of staff were Joan Keighley (later Joan Jenkins) the assistant warden and Penny Condry, the first of a series of volunteer cooks. In the first year none of the jobs were paid.

It was up to Peter to consolidate and expand the good work started by John Fursdon in the first year. Only two small traps had been rebuilt the previous year, one in the garden and the house trap. It was left to him, with the help of visitors, to build the big Heligoland trap. This was a hit or miss affair, for no-one had any plans and no-one had ever seen one. As a result it was made too big, nor was the shape correct. It did not have a big enough angle in the middle so that a keen-eyed bird could see straight through the glass of the catching box. A sparrow-hawk, which flew into the wide mouth of the trap, was seen to fly straight through and out the other end, smashing the glass en route.

Post-war food rationing was still in force, so they collected gulls' eggs every day. For egg-collecting purposes the island was divided, with the lighthouse keepers taking those in the west and the observatory those to the east. Peter comments that he had little doubt that this collecting was effective in controlling gull numbers; it was notable that when egg rationing ceased gull numbers increased considerably.

Cooking was done on a Primus stove and Rippingilles paraffin heaters, on which a portable oven could be placed. After Calor gas was introduced the oven was used as an incubator by someone working on herring gull chicks. Beds were largely ex-Army and much of the furniture in the common room was made by the Baron. The wheel of the *Alice Williams* had been taken to Lockley's Island Farm and it was some time before he could be persuaded to part with it. Meanwhile Peter put up a wheelbarrow wheel in its place, which he comments earned him some nasty looks. So ended Peter Conder's first year.

On his return the following spring a large number of so called rat faeces were found, so everyone was dosed with .5 grammes of sulpha guanadine as a precautionary measure. There have been other rat scares from time to time over the years, but so far these have proved to be groundless. It is to be hoped they remain so for, if the rats ever got a hold, the devastation to ground-nesting birds would be catastrophic.

Caroline the cow had overwintered on the island and was found to be dry and in poor condition. On the first afternoon one of the sheep came up to the house but fled at the sight of a human being. Winter storm damage was confined to half the roof having been blown off the Baron's workshop.

A further insight into island life is gleaned from the comment that 'the diet is somewhat unvaried and consists mainly of rabbits, badly mangled by Badger, D.C.S.'s dog'.

Peter Conder doing the rounds last thing at night found the kitchen door open and shut it. Next morning when the cook went to prepare the breakfast she found that he had shut Caroline the cow in for the night. 'Many stores were eaten', which is perhaps not surprising seeing that she must have been half starved all winter. A period of storms set in and the boat could not get across so, one way and another, rations got short.

There must be a question as to the numbers of domestic animals on the island. We know about the cow and twenty-one Soay sheep were counted on 1 April, but there is also mention of a young billy goat that fell down a cliff and got stuck.

Bird recording and ringing was the major activity during those early post-war years. The Heligoland trap at the well was in constant use; so was the garden trap. Ringing was not however confined to those caught in the traps as the entry for 18 June 1947 shows:

'After the postponement of the proposed ringing of Shearwaters the previous night, owing to inclement weather, excitement ran high among we visitors assembled in the Common Room at the prospect of venturing out this morning.

'Despite the fact that rain was falling at the time, it was decided to brave the elements and accept a wetting if necessary. One of the visitors was deputised to wake us up at 1 A.M.

'Full of zest and excitement we did out job well and truly, ringing in all 212 Shearwaters in the space of an hour and a half, the majority of which were caught in the vicinity of the lighthouse.

'We were fortunate in that it had stopped raining. Having used up the allotted number of rings for the occasion on the Shearwaters, the Warden decided to try his luck at catching and ringing adult gulls.

'A council of war was held and we were told to follow the Warden and his lady assistant in total darkness to the haunts of the nesting gulls; way over the plateau in the direction of The Stack. There at a given signal all were to dash forward with torches ablaze, grabbing hold of any gull that was found to be nesting there.

'Both the Warden and his assistant went forward in the manner of marathon walkers. At one time they must have received training as night fighters, judging by the manner in which they picked their way in the darkness over low walls, rabbit warrens and rough grass. It required great effort to keep close up to them, by the grace of God we managed to avoid broken limbs.

'After what seemed an endless journey the command was given to 'Charge' forward with torches ablaze. The gulls were there as anticipated, but certainly not asleep, despite the fact that it was 3 a.m. The result was that the gulls were far too quick for us and apart from the Warden, who caught one, the rest of us drew a blank.

'A further consultation took place and it was decided to repeat the operation in the field to the rear of the Farmhouse, near the pond.

'Again a marathon cross country dash took place, again the command "Charge", again the Warden was the only one successful in making a "kill".

'Finally we wended our way homeward, tired but contented, happy in the knowledge of what we had accomplished. Thus ended the beginning of an instructive, exciting and unforgettable morning, which was followed by a perfect day.'

Log entry by C. H. England

Aims and ideals alter over the years; present-day Wardens would throw up their hands in horror and in all likelihood order the visitor off the island, if the circumstances of the following entry were to be repeated:

'The writer spent an exhausting afternoon in a state of excitement on the rocks of Mad Bay with four feet of wire. This he succeeded in putting round the legs of four Razorbills and one Puffin, all of which escaped. Though the hook was narrowed, no further contacts were made. The community of birds were put thoroughly on edge by a figure slithering over the rocks with a ring between its teeth'.

Although he never again took up permanent residence, Lockley was a frequent visitor and was still involved in island management, occasionally staying overnight, as the following entries written by him show:

'In 1939 Skokholm was covered with a thick mat of grass and herbage, following the near extermination of rabbits by cyanogas. In the war years however the rabbit population returned to a climax figure of c.6000 in the autumn of 1945 and the herbage was reduced to a minimum. The wet summer of 1946 and the severe winter following seem to have reduced the rabbits to below normal spring level. The result is that aided by a wet spring the herbage is now unusually luxuriant and the presence of flowering heads of white clover, in great number over the island, is striking to an ex-islander and farmer.

Bracken has encroached approximately at the rate of one yard per annum since 1939 in all directions, except down the cliff slopes and in the rocky areas. The increase in hogweed may be due to a succession of wet years – it was formerly confined to an area near the buildings. A noticeable decrease in the number of breeding gulls as well as Razorbills and Guillemots; but Puffins, Shearwaters and Petrels are unchanged. There has been an increase in open land birds, Meadow Pipits, Wheatears and Skylarks and a decrease in cover breeders, Dunnock and Blackbird.

It is a pleasure to feel that the observations begun here before the war are going on so well and so intensively.'

Another entry in another hand states that: 'R.M.L. left the house at 4.15 a.m. to observe Puffins in Crab Bay. About 7 a.m. he shot a Soay Ram and was helped skin the same by one of the Lighthouse Keepers. Ruth cooked the liver for lunch and we all waded in'.

There are frequent mentions of Caroline the cow and sporadic attempts to get milk out of her, which not surprisingly were unsuccessful, firstly because she had gone dry during the winter and secondly because she did not have a calf, this being a necessary preliminary to milk production, after a cow has been allowed to go dry. Female goats on the contrary will often produce milk without first having a kid, so presumably they thought that cows would do the same.

She had a habit of making friendly advances on visitors, which were often misinterpreted. Peter Conder lost count of the number of times he had to rescue damsels in distress from rock outcrops, to which they had retreated to escape the attentions of the over-zealous Caroline. One way and another she was becoming an embarrassment.

The final entry for the year written on 4 October 1947 says that: 'The boat arrived bringing the Lockley Family, the staff from Dale Fort, three day visitors and the butcher. Caroline was slaughtered on South Haven steps and very quickly cut up. After this the house was closed up, the boat left and the observatory was closed for the winter.'

ABOVE: Razorbills and BELOW: guillemots.

ABOVE: Puffin hide at Crab Bay, Spy Rock in background. BELOW: Mad cow Caroline.

DOWN AMONG THE SEAL HOLES

The logs of the immediate post-war years may not be a good read in the 'popular' sense, but they do give a good picture of life on the island and the scientific studies carried out. They were written up every day, often on a rota system either by the visitors or, in their absence, by the Warden or other island staff.

Wind direction and speed were recorded at 0830, 1300, 1800, and 2200 hours. Temperatures, maximum and minimum, and the movements of the barometer are faithfully set down. Unusual birds are mentioned, as are the arrivals of the first auks and hirundines.

Bird trapping and ringing were carried out daily without fail and everybody was press-ganged into helping catch any rarity that turned up, by driving it into one of the traps. The numbers of birds ringed was phenomenal. For instance, on a typical day there were ringed: one reed warbler, three oystercatcher chicks, one greater black back gull chick, twenty-eight herring gull chicks, one razorbill, twenty-one storm petrels and sixty shearwaters. Shearwaters were the majority of birds ringed during the season and there were frequent ringing forays in the early hours of the morning.

Most visitors came to see the birdlife out of general interest, but serious scientific studies were carried out; notably Joan Keighley on oystercatchers and razorbills, Mary Gillham and Gordon Goodman on ecological studies of the Pembrokeshire islands, Mark Williamson on spiders, Miles Williamson on butterfly migration, Elizabeth Gynn on plant colonisation and more recently Denbigh Vaughan on storm petrels.

Courses of a general nature were and still are a popular attraction. The following log entries record the appreciation and comments of the visitors.

'Once again Mr Lockley came in the Pembroke Petrel to take people for a cruise around Skomer and St Brides Bay, but as dinner was on we couldn't really go. A vital task, the digging of the Elsan 'ole was completed and I hope it will last for the rest of the season.

'In the afternoon I went down on the rope, aided by a team of strong visitors and ringed eighteen nestling Guillemots on a single ledge in Mad Bay.

'In the late evening we decided to have a really good go at the Shearwaters and we did, ringing a total of 302 birds. Bed at 4 a.m., once again several "Long John Silvers", (sic) were found.

41

'I have spent the day with my pockets full of glass specimen tubes full of creepy crawlies swimming around in salty water. I sat on a rock and spent the rest of the morning wondering why I felt water trickling down my legs. As you may have guessed I cracked a tube when I sat down on the rocks.

'Other enjoyable things that have happened to me so far: I have cracked my cranium soundly on the top of the cookhouse door, I've slid most of the way down Crab Bay on my behind and had a red hot time. I've been bombed by a dirty Herring Gull and if that wasn't enough I was chain ganged into helping lug three tons of sand and cement on to a boat on the mainland and lugging it off again on the jetty. Needless to say I got clogged up with cement.

'Apart from these unfortunate incidents I have enjoyed myself immensely. I admire Mike, Chris and Uriel. And especially Alistair and his cooking. Mike's wife brightened the place up and I would like to thank them all.'

D. Foster

'The final interesting observation was made before breakfast, when a Trinity House vessel unloaded oil supplies for the lighthouse. Reflecting on this at breakfast time, the Warden hurriedly left the table to pack the corpse of an Oystercatcher – which had died the previous day of a viral disease – in a cardboard box for despatch by post for scientific investigation.

'However on emerging from the packing station he regretfully observed that the vessel was already under weigh. As a result the Oystercatcher was deposited in the fridge amongst other more palatable organic remains.'

As the following entry shows, after numerous unsuccessful attempts had been made to catch gulls, pride could at time be dented by the amateur's casual approach:

'Soon after lunch T.H.V. *Patricia* anchored in South Haven to disembark the Elder Brethren for the annual inspection of the lighthouse. The Lighthouse men, Dick, Fred and Ivor were in their Sunday best and a fine sight it looked. In the middle of all this we suddenly saw a sailor with three Herring Gulls in his hand. On enquiry he said "I just gottem up thar" and pointing to Alice Knoll he put us to shame.'

Skokholm has a number of caves, which are not easy to find. Anybody thinking of carrying out caving expeditions is strongly advised not to go alone; as the following experiences indicate.

'17th September 1948.
Three female visitors investigated the Seal hole. The Seal hole consists of a series of narrow caves off East Bay. Two cows and a

42

bull seal swam into the caves indulging in much snorting and moaning. The most foolhardy of us pushed through a narrow hole in the caves and there got stuck, being eventually rescued by the remaining two with the aid of a rope after a cool inter cave swim.

'Later
A caving expedition was carried out this afternoon, investigating Pamela's cave in Calf Bay. The entrance to this is below water level, except at very low tide. The cliff having been negotiated, the hole has to be entered, a process involving crawling in corkscrew manner through extremely wet water. A few brave spirits squirmed through the narrow, low roofed exit from the first cave and reported that the passage led into other caves. The remainder of the party accepted this statement as true and most members retired to dry off, before resuming more normal activities.

'10th September 1952.
During the past few days seals have been noticed in a bay between Gallery Point and South Gallery Point. We explored this area during the afternoon as there appeared to be a seal hole here, as the seals dived and then disappeared. There are two caves here, the left hand one is best approached down a chimney in the cliff which brings one out on a rock slightly above the cave and just inside, a rope is then necessary to get down into it.

'After a bit we managed to get down. While we were climbing down a seal appeared and entered the cave, but came out and crash dived on being disturbed and was not seen again. The cave goes in about fifty yards, mostly full of large boulders with a small cleft at the end, full of smaller stones; it smelt strongly of seals.

'We had hoped the next cave could be approached through this, but the only connection was a small cleft through which seal cries could be heard. The other cave, best approached from Gallery Point, was very small but there appears to be an underwater entrance that might be partly uncovered in a spring tide. Though even today, six days after the lowest tide, it was covered. There was definitely a seal inside there by the noises. The cave, provided there is one, is impossible to access under normal conditions. The suggested name for the left hand cave, as it appears to be unnamed is Chimney Cave.'

Accompanied by Graham Thompson – the Warden – Steve Sutcliffe, Sam Robins, Dai Rogers and myself, all of us Skokholm veterans in the 1997 work party spent the best part of an afternoon looking and failing to find the Gallery Point caves. It is possible we were looking too far to the south; we did find a wide-mouthed cave round the corner from Gallery Point, but nothing to match the 1952 description.

Similarly we looked at the Seal Cave in East Bay. What we found nowhere matched the 1948 description of the cave. Either there have been substantial rock falls or, what is more likely, a confusion of place-names. There is a satisfactory seal cave in Peter's Bay and Spider Cave on the south side of Peter's Bay more nearly matches the 1948 description of the East Bay cave.

We also took advantage of the low tides to visit the three caves in Purple Cove. This was the first time I had done this and I realised that, after sixteen years and numerous visits to the island, Skokholm still had many undiscovered marvels to show me.

I mentioned this to Jack Donovan, the chairman of the Islands Management Committee, when I came off. He immediately gave me a right bawling out for, among other things, disturbing the bats that he imagines roost there. How in the world he thinks bats could survive, even in a modest westerly blow, I cannot imagine.

It is more than likely that there are many caves still to be discovered, for the rock formations on the west side would indicate this to be the case. Because the birds nesting on the ledges, the usual rough state of the sea and the precipitous nature of the cliffs all combine to discourage exploration, their secrets must remain a while longer.

As well as the spectacular cliffs and scenery, there are many smaller marvels to discover, as a course member on Shoreline Crustacea relates in the following poem:

'Chatty Log entry 2nd October 1964.

If you go for a walk by the seaside
You may see a sort of a lump
That looks like a kind of a Camel
That's buried right up to its hump.

And if you can creep up behind it
And give it a rather sly kick
You might find, if fortune is with you
The object will deign to unstick.

Oh! Did I say fortune on your side?
Your troubles have only begun;
You've just found a nice little limpet.
The question my friend, is 'Which One?'

Take a look at the foot that it walks on
And see if it's orange or grey;
You will find that the answer won't help you
In spite of what all the books say.

You will need the most remarkable eyesight
To see its tentacular fringe:
Make a note if it's white or transparent
Or is it more of a creamier tinge?

Now if you are rather a rotter
And have with you a suitable knife
You can gouge out the poor little creature
(Such a wanton destruction of life).

But crawl out from under your conscience
And measure the length of its tongue
Then look in the shell you've just dug out
For the scar where the limpet once hung.

It may be a sort of bright orange
That varies to rather dark grey
Or, if you read different textbooks
It varies the opposite way.

So you see it's excessively simple
No! - - - - - - Don't stamp your foot like a child;
You have dropped the darn thing in the water –
Well there's really no need to get wild.

If you go for a walk by the seaside
Don't trouble the limpets at play.
Its really far kinder to leave them
And they won't have to lock you away!

(I am told that a far better method
Of being sent clean off you head
Is to steer clear of littoral fauna
And try to catch rabbits instead)'

Godfrey L. Crewe

ABOVE: Seals on the rocks in South Haven.
BELOW: Weather conditions and temperatures are
regularly recorded.

The caves in Purple Cove, with figures at base of
cliff. (Photo by Graham Thompson)

LEFT: The entrance to East Bay cave and RIGHT: Dai Rogers exploring Spider Cave. BELOW: A member of the rapidly expanding fulmar colony and RIGHT: a rare sighting of a group of turnstones.

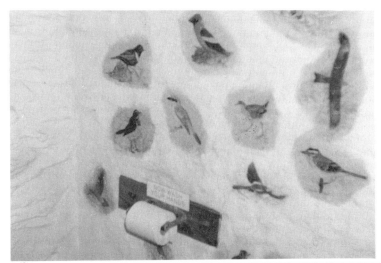

ABOVE: Visitors are encouraged to record sightings of rare birds where everyone can see them, in the loo. BELOW: Oystercatchers on the Anticline roost.

49

ABOVE: The buildings from the south east.
BELOW: Looking towards Hog Bay. Wreck Cove is
the other side of the headland. *Alice Williams* can
just be seen on The Knoll.

CROWNING GLORIES

1953 was the Coronation year of Her Majesty the Queen and, while the work of the observatory continued as usual, the day was not allowed to pass without appropriate celebrations. The log entry for Sunday 31 May 1953 reads as follows:

'Preparations for the Coronation festivities continued apace. Peter and Ron manhandled several loads of driftwood up to the bonfire on Spy Rock. Commander Sholto Douglas sallied forth with a gleam in his eye and the .22 in his hand; he returned with Three Greater Black back Gulls and one Lesser Black back. It is intended to prepare these magnificent corpses for the Coronation feast, outdoing James II who had to be content with cold Puffins, according to the *Daily Express.* (The Lesser Black back was shot by mistake).

'The ladies of the party spent the day, when they weren't preparing the G.B.B.'s for the Coronation feast and bashing the flesh (on Ronald Lockley's advice) to make it tender, in observing wildlife around the island.

'After supper I spent a desperate hour trying to provide an alternative menu for tomorrow's "G.B.B. a la Coronation" and at last achieved three rabbits out of eight shots.

'I feel that tomorrow will be quite a day with bonfire and G.B.B. in spite of no papers or wireless.'

While the rest of the country was generally junketing around and making whoopee for the Coronation of Her Majesty, life on Skokholm continued more or less as normal, with their own celebrations fitted in as best could be. The log entry for the day is reproduced in full.

'CORONATION DAY Tuesday June 2nd 1953.

'Weather: Wind N.N.W. force 6 moderating a little in evening. Showery at first becoming brighter, COLD.

Birds Ringed. 7 Oystercatcher Nestlings. *Birds Recovered.* 2 Shearwaters. *Bird Movements.* None.

'General Activities.
As usual the day's activities began soon after midnight with Geoffrey's experimental work, which he continued with Evelyn's aid – but only two new recoveries were made. [What the experimental work was is not recorded. Presumably the two recoveries were the two Shearwaters mentioned above].

'The morning was wet and windy, so without any previous intention the party found themselves in the Common Room just before 11 a.m. Paula brought in tea and Peter brought in the wireless set. We followed the Coronation broadcast until lunch time and loyally drank to Queen Elizabeth, after her crowning, in sherry thoughtfully provided by John Moyse.

'The chief question of the lunch was provided by the question– who could manage to eat G.B.B. flesh? Surprisingly most of the party tasted it and several thought it not unpleasant, although an even slower cooking might have removed the suggestion of sawdust in its texture. A few unenterprising males preferred rabbit. Both were eclipsed by the apricot pudding, which Paula had made, washed down with Gin and Orange, which Geoffrey had carefully shepherded across in the boat.

'The afternoon was sunny but the wind was too high to produce many interesting bird records. Ron hoped to lead an expedition to the Stack, but although the ladder was carried down to the verge, it was decided that the wind was high enough to carry away both ladder and passenger, so the attempt was reluctantly postponed. The Commander then continued with his hooked wire to *observe* Razorbills, rather than to catch them!

'The writer looked for other types of fauna and finds included three eels, less than four inches long in Orchid Stream and a count of three out of six male slow worms showing blue spots.

'For our evening meal we tasted the produce of the garden – new potatoes and lettuce. Soon after dark the party completed its celebrations by climbing to Spy Rock and lighting the bonfire and watching other bonfires on the mainland. At least six could be seen and fireworks rose from the Dale area. Could they see us?

'It is probable that the returning party, cold from the high wind, will be warmed with rum – which Geoffrey has also produced, but this record must be finished before its effects are felt.'

Whether it happened on this occasion or some other, the log is more than reticent and the writer has had to rely on strong rumours from other sources.

'On High days and Holidays, excursions used to be run on the light railway from South Haven to the Lighthouse. Stops were made at "Puffin Halt", Garden Rocks and other places of interest. On one occasion the brakes failed, according to the official explanation, on the return journey. Unofficially the driver and passengers were so inebriated that they let the thing get out of control. Gathering speed the trolley crashed into the buffers at South Haven, everything got smashed to pieces and finished up on the rocks below. Fortunately passengers and crew cast themselves off in time and no-one witnessed the final crash.'

ABOVE: Buildings seen from The Neck. BELOW:
Meals are served in The Wheelhouse with the
Warden at the head of the table.

53

ABOVE: A well preserved section of stone wall,
built in a unique herringbone fashion. BELOW:
Prof Christopher Perrins demonstrates a spotted
crake to the management committee, David
Stanbury with the pipe in the left background.

OF SHEEP AND GOATS

It seems that Skokholm was extensively farmed at some time and Lockley mentions a Captain Harrison and his five daughters who occupied the island in the mid-nineteenth century. They had ten cows, grew cereals, had pigs and sheep and several plough teams. Supporting this view are the remains of the walls dividing the different fields, which would have been much more prominent than they are today, if they were to be stockproof. They certainly represent a great deal of labour and are themselves an indication that the island was once a viable farm, maybe not in today's accepted sense, but capable of supporting a family in less demanding times.

There are signs on the Northern Plain, and the meadows in front of and behind the buildings, that these fields were once ploughed. When Lockley negotiated the taking over of the lease from 'Bulldog' Edwards, he was told that Skokholm grew 'Wunnerful crops of Oats' and the seed was in great demand on the mainland.

Other than a few vegetables in the garden and a potato patch above where the *Alice Williams* used to stand overlooking South Haven, Lockley grew no crops. Instead he relied on sheep for the main source of his income and mentioned that the island was capable of supporting between fifty and a hundred ewes.

Some indication of the island's grazing potential may be judged from an entry in March 1950 which recorded that Soay triplets were reported from the Head and – 'we have already found at least three pairs of twins'. Twins and triplets do not come from poor quality grazing.

Then of course there were the goats, which numbered about twelve. To improve the strain Peter Conder bought a goat in kid from the lighthouse, which poses the question whose goats were they, and were there two flocks? Another entry states that the lighthouse keepers shot their billy goat because he was becoming dangerous. He must have been a tough old fellow because it took five shots at point blank range to finish him off!

In lighter vein – Joe, a visiting carpenter, wondered where the milk came from and was invited to see the rabbits milked that evening! 'David made eleven "rabbit stalls" out of an orange box and Gwen – the originator of the whole business – prepared the "milking machine", out of the rubber part of an old scent spray. After tea she prepared some "rabbits milk", (dilute goats milk) and even warmed it just as Joe was seen approaching. Joe swallowed the whole thing and even took some rabbit's milk back with him.

'Next day it was reported that "The Skipper" was well pleased with the demonstration given to Joe of rabbit milking. Even though he had seen it all Joe still firmly refused to have rabbit's milk in his tea.'

An early task in 1953 was the building or refurbishment of the slipway, originally built by Lockley, in the valley to the left of the track leading up from the landing. This was so that *Swallow*, the island boat, could be hauled up clear of the waves. Peter Conder had once had a nasty experience when he took a friend fishing. The wind dropped and they started to drift towards America, someone spotted them from the Lighthouse and they had to be rescued by an Air-Sea Rescue launch.

The winds and currents round the island can be tricky and, as will be seen later, the author had a similar experience on a 'round the island' trip.

Peter Conder's bow and arrows are frequently mentioned, also that on one occasion he shot four rabbits, so he must have been a pretty nifty shot. On another occasion he was 'severely censured' for shooting a pigeon that was eating the radishes in his garden.

The year 1953 also saw the arrival of Messrs Powell to build a new laboratory. This was on the site of the present laboratory and remained until the whole of the central block of buildings was enlarged and rebuilt in 1987.

Ringing continued to be the main activity and it is recorded that on 8 May 1953 they ringed fifteen whitethroats, twelve sedge warblers and three willow warblers, one of which was of the northern race. A considerable amount of effort was also expended descending to guillemot ledges for ringing purposes.

The goats made their presence felt on occasions. When the billies fell out with each other, one was banished to Midland Island. Ivanhoe, the chief billy, was still a nuisance, so he was taken down to the quay and slaughtered by Harold Sturley and John Barrett.

Obviously the goats enjoyed teasing the Wardens, because on another occasion pity was taken on three goats apparently stranded on a ledge in Wreck Bay. Valiant attempts to rescue them were made by trying to lassoo them and haul them up, but the Wardens were not all that handy with a lassoo. The goats got tired of the game and walked up effortlessly on their own.

As was usual the first day of the Wardens' return in 1954 was taken up in cleaning and decorating. The lighthouse dumper was not always available and the stores had to be carried up from the landing on stretchers. Bringing water to the buildings was another thankless chore and, to lighten the tedious task, races with full buckets were organised.

After a long and successful stewardship, during which he did valuable research on wheatears, Peter Conder retired as Warden and was succeeded by Peter Davis, who had previously been on Lundy Island. The occasion of his departure was marked by a sherry party in the Common Room, at which the honours were done by Colonel Brownlow. Peter went on to be the Deputy Director and eventually Director of the RSPB. His services to ornithology were recognised by the award of an OBE in 1976.

No doubt anxious to make his mark, the new Warden pressed on with the ringing programme – stormies, puffins and on 24 August they ringed 248 shearwaters and ran out of rings.

The autumn of 1954 was spent by the Warden re-building Half Way House, incorporating Caroline's cowshed. This would have been half way along the Middle Block abutting on to what we now call the Bull Pen. It served as the Warden's quarters for many years. He also started building Cook's Cottage, which must have been the space now occupied by the larder.

There was no boat for fifteen days, the food situation became desperate and the Warden shot a Soay sheep. He had to shoot another three weeks later, the skins being used as a hearthrug for Cook's Cottage.

Much more use was made of the island's natural food supply. Sea beet from the Stack is recorded as being a delicacy, as were gull's eggs when available. Their lack of knowledge of fungi however got them into trouble, because several members became ill after eating parasol mushrooms.

In early 1956 a part of six landed for a three week stay, the object being a trapping exercise using humane rabbit traps. This followed a survey by Ministry of Agriculture officers the previous autumn. A cold spell set in and hard frost and snow froze the traps solidly to the ground. However, their time was not entirely wasted, after a week's labour, even though they only caught ten rabbits; they caught 86 mice in the Wheelhouse.

The resident staff at the time were Peter and Angela Davis and cook Pauline. They record that they heard many ducks on the ponds during the evenings, mainly wigeon.

On 28 March 1956 a start was made on building a pig sty to accommodate one small porker, provided by Harold Sturley and due to arrive on the Saturday boat. This took rather longer than expected and the pig had to be turned loose in the Wheelhouse compound, where his antics kept everyone amused. Objecting loudly, he was eventually confined to the woodshed. After a few days the pig sty was completed and the pig – with considerable difficulty – was transported to its new home.

There was never a dull moment with Samson, which is what he was christened. During the night Sugarback, the island pony, got into the compound and ate Samson's breakfast. He retaliated by getting out of his sty and, after a long search, was found in Hog Bay.

An early project for the year was to run an iron pipe from the well up to the buildings. On 7 April, after a great deal of labour on the pump, a tablespoonful of water trickled out into the tank. Because of the distance and the lift involved, the scheme was never a success and was abandoned in favour of more basic methods until the present ram was installed in 1986.

Another fortnight went by and Samson again escaped and, after another long search, was found sun-bathing on Spy Rock. Two days later he escaped twice and wire netting was added to his pen.

An abandoned lamb was attracted by the gulls and after unsuccessful efforts to find its Mum it was reluctantly adopted by Angela. It was christened Kelly, after Grace, Princess of Monaco, but was later found to be a ram. Gulls attacking lambs was quite a common occurrence.

Samson left for the mainland on 15 May, whether because they were fed up with him or he was going for the *coup-de-grace* I know not. A few days later there is a note that he had arrived at Dale safely and been sent to market.

Evidently they decided to persevere with pigs because a fortnight later two more turned up on the boat. One was a handsome young boar and the other a diminutive runt 'thrown in' by the vendor, 'to see what we could do with it'. The larger of the two pigs was also named Samson and eight weeks later he also left for market. Simpson, the other one, prolonged his stay until the end of the year. Around the same time a Toggenburg billy goat was brought over 'to improve the strain'.

Two sheep were shot and dressed, 'they provided an enormous fry of liver and kidney'. The carcasses were cut up and packed in salt for mainland use, presumably to feed the Wardens during the winter, for island pay would not have gone far on the mainland and who can blame them for looking after number one. In all a total of seventeen animals – ten rams and seven ewes – were killed between June and October; one other died and the flock, which numbered 72 at the end of the lambing season, now numbered 54. Presumably they had to fend for themselves during the winter.

1957 was notable for happenings in the animal world. On 2 April a small female pig christened Delilah arrived. The sty had been refurbished to accommodate her but not that successfully, because it was not long before the Wardens discovered what good bulldozers pig's snouts make. Delilah escaped and, after the best part of a day's search, was found on Spy Rock.

The Soay sheep flock started lambing on 4 April, by producing two sets of twins. By 4 May the count was 14 rams, 44 ewes and at least 16 lambs. The fact that Skokholm could support this number of sheep, plus an unknown quantity of goats indicates that the rabbits must have been kept well under control. The island certainly could not support anything like such a number under present-day conditions and there is no record of any winter supplementary feeding. The island's grazing potential is readily apparent, when note is taken of the amount and quality of vegetation in the rabbit exclosures.

The Soay is an extremely hardy sheep and can live on little, but even so there must have been casualties, even in a mild winter. From my own experience on St Kilda, where there is also a Soay flock, the first task in the spring is to organise a burial party. Otherwise there would have been loud complaints from the visitors. Oddly there is no record of Skokholm casualties, but there must have been some.

Whether the sheep flock was managed or whether it was left to its own devices is an open question. Even if a few ewes were late lambing it seems half of them were barren. Fourteen rams were left on the island, whereas two should have been ample to cover a flock that size. Apart from a hint that the flock was managed and presumably owned by West Wales Field Society, no-one seems to know the answer to these questions or whether they were dipped regularly.

The pony Sugarback was another animal that had to fend for himself and during hard winters he must have found it hard going. Unlike the Soay, horses are unable to live on next to nothing. He had been brought to the island to haul carriages on the light railway, which ran from South Haven to the Lighthouse. With the arrival of the dumper truck his services were no longer required and he was left to his own devices.

When the Wardens returned to the island in the spring he was not surprisingly in poor condition and could not move far. On 5 May he was found dead and he was buried with great ceremony on the edge of South Bog. A concrete slab suitably inscribed marks the spot. It must have been a sad end for an island favourite.

The Ministry of Agriculture was interested in Skokholm, which indicates that a regular return was made on the island's potential as a farm, hence the Soay sheep flock. On 24 June a party from the Ministry visited the island, with the result that three rabbit trappers were sent over in the autumn and stayed for a month. It is more than likely that whoever was in charge was told that they must make some effort to reduce the rabbit population and improve the grazing, to qualify for a marginal land grant.

It has to be remembered that at that time the whole country was at the tail-end of wartime controls on land use, designed to maximise food production from every available acre.

Parties from Dale Fort were frequent visitors and there is a record of an invasion of students one morning. Five were capable of work but the remainder were either seasick, or anticipated being sea sick on their return. Kipper sandwiches for lunch did not seem to improve matters!

By the end of the year, 7,000 birds had been ringed and, when the Wardens finally closed the island for the winter, Rupert the pig departed in their company. Also leaving were Peter and Angela Davis, who went to take up a post in Fair Isle. They were succeeded as Wardens by George Edwards.

1958 got off to a cold start. Four and a half inches of snow were recorded on 9 March and by next day it had increased to six. We wonder how the Soay flock coped with that.

Cold easterlies continued during the whole of March and, even though the weather was cold, romance was hot, because Dido the cook got engaged to Einar the Danish assistant Warden on 6 April, the engagement ring appropriately being Shearwater ring No 54500.

Bird ringing continued apace and it is worth mentioning for it shows the scale of activity and the numbers of some birds that are not so common nowadays.

On 17 July 423 were ringed: 283 shearwaters, one oystercatcher, 10 lesser black-backed gulls, one herring gull, two kittiwakes, 19 razorbills, 56 guillemots, 44 puffins, one wheatear, five rock pipits and one shag. On 21 August they ringed 215 willow warblers, 12 spotted flycatchers, seven whitethroats, one garden warbler, one sedge warbler and three wheatears. The year's total was 8,300 birds. At least another 392 were ringed during the year.

Ringing does seem to have come a fanatical obsession and there is one mention of shearwaters being dug out of burrows! One shudders to think what mayhem must have been caused by descending to guillemot ledges for ringing.

Log entries for this time are almost wholly confined to meteorological records, bird movements and ringing. An indication that the Wardens and visitors were still living off the land is indicated on 30 March 1959, by a note that George and Dan picked out a sheep to shoot. Before they could take aim the flock they were watching was chased by three goats.

May 1959 was also notable for two other events. On the 16th there was the first visit of Forest Hill School, led by their Headmaster David Stanbury. This started a long association with

David, who became a valued member of the management committee and historical researcher of the island.

The other event of note was that on 27 May the 100,000th bird was ringed – a storm petrel.

The individual record for numbers ringed was yet to come and happened in 1966. This was when Chris Perrins – later Professor Christopher Perrins, director of the Edward Grey Institute for Field Studies – aided by his family, ringed over 1,000 shearwater pulli in one night and over 10,000 pulli in the year.

Getting back to the sheep, apart from those that were shot for food, it appears that the flock was culled from time to time. An entry on 7 February 1960, concerning a winter visit, mentions that there was no sign of any sheep. This is not particularly surprising because Soay are adept at hiding in gulleys down a cliff face. The entry reads:

'We heard later that the West Wales Field Society had removed all but ten, but it seems remarkable that these were not seen.' There is no further mention of sheep in the logs or when they were finally all evacuated. But Jean Lawman recalls that there was one running with the goats in 1976.

Sugarback in happier days.

LEFT: Jim Poole standing in the Skokholm sheep
dip tank. RIGHT: The old dumper truck, Serial No
1? BELOW: View from the Lighthouse, looking
east.

62

COMINGS AND GOINGS

When a building project is in hand and quantities of heavy materials have to be lifted on to the island, the state of the tide, the weather or sheer cussedness on the part of the boatman all seem to work against those who have to do the donkey work. Thus the following heartfelt entry in the log, written by an unknown hand. '27th August 1961.

'*Cubango* appeared in South Haven and then the fun started. It was one of the lowest tides of the year and it was right out. So low in fact that the boat ran aground trying to come alongside the rocks. The jetty itself was way back, almost out of sight. The engine was put at full astern, Reuben Codd heaved on the boat hook, but she remained stuck fast. The result was that Don Glanville – the Warden – Dave and myself had to jump in the drink fully clothed and push her off.

'Then began the awful task of unloading, as it was obvious the boat would not come alongside. As luck would have it Reuben brought over several hundredweight of sand and cement, great pieces of asbestos roofing, plus timber and tools; all of which had to be unloaded on to our backs from the bows of the boat, as we stood waist high in the water. We had to stumble back with it to dry land, getting mixed up with seaweed and rocks in the process. Then came the visitors luggage and lastly the poor folks themselves, who luckily – the tide having come in a bit in the meantime – were able to jump on the slippery sharp rocks. The visitors going off followed in likewise fashion. After a few narrow escapes and barked shins, all and sundry were safely aboard and with John Barrett laughing all over his face the boat finally went astern and departed for Dale Fort.

'The last job was humping all the stores and building material over the rocks into the waiting dumper. The rest of the day was rather an anti-climax with a late lunch, a later supper and late cocoa.'

Boat arrivals always engender a certain amount of excitement and on some occasions can be a mixed blessing, as the following entry indicates:

'27th Mary 1962

The day was rather chilly and it rained for a while. The big event of the day happened after lunch when Penny came with the message that Peter had probably broken his leg in Crab Bay. No brandy was found, the stretcher nuts were rusty and no sticks of the right size were found. When we all hurried to Spy Rock a boat appeared and I was sent to the jetty to ask it to hold on. It was a party of about twelve people and when I told the Captain what I knew he said he said he was going to Crab Bay with the boat. I said he couldn't, but was told by a startled woman that it was Mr Lockley himself and I should have known he was a V.I.P.

'The party wanted to see the houses and walked up the slope. In the meanwhile Peter was brought into the Common Room. He hadn't broken anything. As it had happened before, Don and Sam asserted their authority and said he had to go with the boat to the mainland.

'The party had gathered on the grass and some of the ladies wanted to know how often the traps were emptied. They wanted them to be checked continually as the poor birds would die in the small glass boxes. The gulls eggs in the Wheelhouse for breakfast, upset them also – cruelty!

'The only two trapped birds of the day were brought in and Don demonstrated ringing. One man wanted to be shown a Chough and a Storm Petrel – so would some of the rest of us!

'Peter was carried down to the boat on a repaired stretcher and Richard rushed up to the Lighthouse to send a message to Dale Fort.

'Two lighthouse men appeared in full uniform as the boat started to leave. The boat didn't leave in the grand style it should have done as Mr Lockley had forgotten to tie the anchor string (sic) to the boat and the spare anchor was gone. They tried to fish it up but in vain. The old ladies were helped on board and we walked up to the house for a well needed cup of tea.

'After supper Zygmunt (research student) started boiling up his stinky old gulls. He'll take the bones back to Poland.

'Don showed his impressive knowledge in reading all the birds names in Latin and soon afterwards he spoke lyrically about his bed and the day was over.'

Another Lockley visit on 14 October 1962 turned out to be far more rewarding:

'Half way through the morning we sighted a launch coming this way, it turned out to be Mr Lockley who kindly asked us if we would like to go with them. We of course jumped at the chance. After calling at Skomer for David Saunders we headed out to sea. We went first to 'The Smalls', circled it but were unable to land because of the state of the tide. We left there and headed back towards Grassholm where we were fortunate enough to land and spend a wonderful hour. We were glad to find many of the Gannets still there and were also lucky enough to see a great variety of migrants. Amongst these were one Common Sandpiper, a Rook, a Woodpigeon, Snow Bunting, a Short Eared Owl and many others. We also saw a large number of seals; but Mr Lockley and party did not manage to catch any until we arrived back at Skomer, where they found and caught two seal pups, we were deposited back on our island after a very enjoyable and eventful day.'

Another exciting day is recorded on 9 May 1964 when the Warden – Mike Harris – arrived from the lighthouse with the hot news that a petrol tanker had stopped off Skomer, with engine trouble, and was being pushed on to the rocks:

'After tea the lighthouse crew arrived in the driving rain and we all watched the drama at sea. By now the tanker, which had been towed by a tug, the *Thorngarth* from Milford, was adrift in the high seas heading at speed for disaster on the rocks of Gateholm. The original cable had snapped after the convoy had reached the lighthouse. The snaking cable breaking one man's arm and splitting another's head. A lifeboat from St David's was also assisting by taking off surplus crew. The remainder were working frantically to remove the old cable and attach another. With only a few minutes to spare before the hoped for explosion – as the petrol blew up – the tug started to tow the *Hostility*, 933 tons unladen, towards Milford and the lifeboat headed for home. The whole convoy was lost to sight as the mists and rain strengthened.'

There was great excitement on another occasion when 'After several days of strong winds the on-coming visitors were relieved to find that the boat was going to make the crossing. For some the relief changed to regret after St Anne's Head was passed and more than one Fort breakfast was sacrificed ere Skokholm was gained.

'Morale was somewhat strengthened when it was discovered that Her Brittanic Majesty was suffering the same seas within a few miles, H.M.S. *Britannia* a-gaggle with flags and dutifully escorted at respectful distance by a Frigate, passed close under the lighthouse soon after midday. The lighthouse duly responded with a flag to show they realised who it was. *Britannia* was en-route from Cardiff to the Hebrides and made rather easier progress, with its multiplicity of stabilisers – than Alf Knowles' other vessel. However Her Majesty had the sincere sympathy of many an observer!'

Coming and goings on Skokholm are – as the visitor quickly discovers – very much dependent on the weather. This is especially so at the beginning and end of the season and, while some may lose out, others may gain, as the following entry shows:

'There was little to commend this day to posterity until the evening, when staff and visitors attained a tremendous spiritual uplift, through the uncanny foresight of Giles and John, who panicked because of Wednesday's gale, departing on Thursday instead of risking being delayed over the weekend. In doing so they left unclaimed a cheerful package containing a bottle of fine liqueur brandy.

'If the foregoing is thought to be unnecessarily long, the volubility must be ascribed to the tonic effects of the weighty decision, which had been debated at every mealtime since *Cubango's* departure, was finally and irrevocably taken at 1000 hours today.

'It was considered that a) bottles break in the post, b) Giles and John were in a much better position to obtain another bottle of vintage brandy, c) it is a bad thing to be exposed to temptation and not succumb to it, d) the relief Warden was obviously in for a stinking cold and his need could be regarded as medicinal, e) since he hates drinking alone, this was a good reason for implicating the others.

'The long and short of it was we broached the bottle and having reduced the level by half felt cosy enough to venture out on a Shearwater hunt. This was not very successful owing to the paucity of Shearwaters and their appearing to have doubles. We hurried home to the other half of the bottle and finished it amidst scenes of indescribable chaos at about 2 a.m.

'Martine's eyes closed about 1.30 a.m. and she was led protesting feebly to the garden room. When she was removed from the Common Room sofa Robert took the line of least resistance and fell unconscious there. Marjorie and Jane floated on high to the Angel Loft and said things which banished Egbert and condemned him to a wet and windy night. The present writer was perfectly sober, as may be seen by his firmness of hand 48 hours later.

'As for the singing that came from the loft, it certainly did not sound like Angels and it kept me awake half the night.

'Though memory is somewhat dimmed, I believe one or two birds and eight Shearwaters were ringed during the day and the weather was really much worse than the preparatory note to today's entry suggests. It is good to have the fortunes of a bird observatory in the palm of one's hand again, especially with a cook like Marty thrown in. And heaven will need to help Skokholm in the days to come.'

ABOVE: Returning from a Lighthouse delivery.
BELOW: Gannets on the *qui vive*.

ABOVE: First landing of the season and it had to be at Blacksmith's. (Photo Theresa Purcell) BELOW: An early Work Party, or is it Shackleton landing on Elephant Island?

HAPPY LANDINGS

No matter how many times you visit or return to the island, the first landing of the season rarely goes to plan and always brings the unexpected. Mike Brook, who was warden from 1973-1976, mentions the usual number of relatively minor incidents, when he returned on 8 March 1975.

'The weather was sufficiently generous to allow the return to the island to be made on the planned Saturday; although only after midday second thoughts from Terry. [Terry Davis, who at that time was running the boat service from Martinshaven]. Even so, unloading with the valuable help of Simon and Bill from the lighthouse was very awkward, so that the sea claimed the 88lb tin of Snowcem, a 7lb tin of Marmalade and all my vegetables. The first two were retrieved unharmed at low tide; the latter fed the crabs and I seemed to spend the first week living on Spaghetti Bolognese. The prospect of catering sized tins of carrots for a month was too daunting.

'Company was provided by Vanilla and Essence, a goat and kid, caught on the first night in the limekiln. Tragedy struck, shortly after Ray and Jean Lawman – the assistant warden and cook – arrived on the 15th. Essence was found mysteriously dead one morning, perhaps he had been squashed by his mother. Although Vanilla more or less tolerated having her nipples handled she refused to deliver up any milk. Nevertheless we have left her tethered so that she is now very friendly, but also extremely thin.

'The buildings were in a tolerable state, no crumbling walls, no algal proliferations and less than ten dead mice. The mould prize went to a biscuit tin containing some of last year's scones, with tea leaves not far behind. At the end of two weeks we have broken the back of scrubbing, snowceming, painting and trap mending.

'The weather has lately been most unseasonable. The first week was grey and cold, the second week was clear and cold with ice on the puddles and even on winter pond. This week has been punctuated by vicious snow and hail showers, which have left the island almost white at times. Such conditions have naturally enough deterred any would-be migrants and the only summer visitor we have seen is a female Wheatear, which stayed for four days.

'Up to five Choughs have been around almost daily – fingers crossed that they will remain to breed. The only rarity has been a

Magpie, the fourth island record. Meanwhile the hens seem to have settled down under the roving eye of the handsome cockerel, who hasn't yet shown much signs of asserting his masculinity. I am pleased to say that his crowing would not win any prizes for its persistence around dawn.

'To get back to the goats. One called Baggins had to be evacuated because he butted the visitors and chewed their haversacks and anoraks.

'The wild goats originally numbered thirteen, minus Baggins equals twelve. The whole herd had been chased into Dip Gully in order to catch Baggins. Veronica has also been caught and now adds further delight to the quantities of wild animals, hens etc provided to keep the visitors amused when no birds are about.

'During the chase Big Billy and two other goats got stuck and had to retreat into a cave as the tide came up. Jim the lighthouse keeper discovered their plight and a great plan was hatched to get them up the cliff. Ray, the stalwart handyman, set about making a goat ladder. Ian the rock climber was seen to approach the rescue zone and got to within fifteen feet of Big Billy when a toss of the head sent him flying backwards, nearly into the sea; but not quite, much to everyone's consternation.

'The ladder was sent to Dip Gully by dumper and everyone sat back to wait for another low tide, so the rescue could be carried out. Big anti-climax, the three goats walked up the cliff and joined the rest of the herd before any rescuers turned up.'

David Stanbury, who has visited the island times without number also has something to say about the boat journey and landing:

'There is one constant feature about the boat journey, it is never the same twice! The new feature this time was a semi abseil down a 100ft cliff with all our luggage, five calor gas cylinders, bursting bags of groceries, sacks of bread and meat and lots of little unauthorised bags of personal goodies. It was also very hot!

'As if all this was not enough, all the gear had to be piled up within reach of the rubber dinghy and also within reach of the incoming tide, on a beach full of weedy boulders. Having got the luggage and stores wet we decided to join them.

'Anyway we finally got this mountain of wet luggage and people on to the boat and went to Skomer. This was to land a few Skomer visitors and to enable the Skomer Warden to have a row with David Saunders. This took a long time, a very long time. In the end the boatman joined in with a little unparliamentary language and we went to Skokholm at last, leaving the disconsolate Skomer Warden preparing a welcome for the Dale Fort boat.

'A warm welcome, a working dumper, out of the wellies and a gin and tonic at long last. It is difficult to describe the impact of the island on a sunny day in early summer. The combination of colours, the rusty red rock, bright orange lichen, deep blue bluebells, vivid pink thrift, yellow primroses, bright green bracken, blue sea and sky, the scarlet crane and the whitewashed landing. The fragrance of scents and smells from the wildflowers, the seaweed washed up in the Haven. The paraffin, the wood smoke, the calor gas, the musky scent of Shearwater burrows and the crushed plants under your feet, the movement of plants in the wind, the slow procession of white clouds across a blue sky, the slip slop surge of the rising tide. The buzz of bees, the whistle of the wind through the cracks in the wall, the clink of loose stones on the path, even the thump of the dumper truck – and then there are the birds, that's why we came to the island. Hundreds of them, thousands, gulls screaming and wheeling overhead. Puffins ducking and diving round the Haven, Oystercatchers piping, skylarks singing in spirals in the sky, blackbirds fluting in the brambles, ravens croaking; a treasury of movement, sound colour and activity.

'Then there are the ancient stone walls, the old lime kiln, the slightly crooked cottage, the cool wheelhouse, the well, the well trodden path, the figurehead, the pile of driftwood, the ghost of Ronald Lockley.

'But even this is not quite Skokholm. It is the people, the memories, the stories, the laughter round the fire, the hiss of the lamps, the animated conversation at the end of the day and those eerie nocturnal shearwater calls gurgling through the night.'

In another hand an entry written at the same time reads as follows:

'The main corporate feature was "stormying" in the late evening. Here again it was the warmest evening I can remember. This is the only occasion I have remembered to bring my duffel coat, and it was quite unnecessary. I believe there is some law – with a rude name – that applies to circumstances such as these. But to continue – the petrel hunt was very satisfying. We saw many as we sat below the lighthouse and others were seen in cracks and crevices. Alas the shearwater section was not a spectacular success – I saw one after a considerable expenditure of torch power. But to be fair to the Warden he had not held out much hope of the shearwaters coming in on such a light night.

'We returned at about midnight. I was pleased that our Tilley lamp was burning well and that those of D.J.S. and J.P. had gone out. So I went to bed to the accompaniment of blundering sounds from neighbouring rooms. All very satisfying.'

71

ABOVE: Ray Lawman finds an orphan goat.
BELOW: A gathering storm over the island.

72

FERTIGAN WEEK

For many years David Stanbury, the then Headmaster of Forest Hill School, London – took a party of pupils and staff to Skokholm. The year of the Queen's Jubilee in 1977 was memorable for the quality of entries the pupils wrote in the Chatty Log and for the adventures therein recorded.

For the reader's sake I have cleaned up the punctuation but the spelling is 'as written' in the log.

'The beginning of Forest Hill week – 4 June 1977.

'Yesterday's log written today 5th June 1977
Mr T. Collins, at risk or life and limb, woke us all up at 5.00. By 5.30 the mini bus (all three of them) were all packed and we were on our way to sunny Marloes. At 8.30 there were quick dashes between the car park and the beach to ferry kit and food straight on to the boat and an easy crossing to Skokholm.

The rest of the day passed quite painlessly, a tour around the island, a lunch devouring session, a walk, football, a dinner devouring session, a walk and coffee and biscuits. Altogether it was a very tiring day – I for one was asleep in five minutes. Points to remember for rest of trip:-

1. There are no Penguins in Crab Bay.
2. No, the noise coming from the south of the island is not a sick whale – its a 'Foghorn'.
3. If T.Collins says 'Sorry', I can't hear you over the hiss of the Tilly lamps', threaten to take away his G & T.

Finally how could Forest Hill School let a great tradition die – the chatty log of all things. Well F.H.S. is back on Skokholm and so too is the Chatty Log.'

Peter Jackson

'5th June 1977, Today's log written today.
Today I woke at 6.30 to hear the noise of the rain pouring and the Foghorn. After falling out of bed to find my watch I climbed back into bed. I then woke at 7.30 and fell asleep.

'Later
After a good-ish breakfast and fiddling the rotor, (washing up rota) I went to Crab Bay, nothing there I thought after seeing nothing. I then walked to the lighthouse after tripping over a

chipping egg. I then got too near the goats which did'nt like it, who insidentally were as frighten and timided as I was.

'Yesterday's log written today 6th June 1977.
I then got very close to Puffins without my camera, so I went back for my camera and they had all gone to see. I then went to find the goats but didn't get near them. I then risked my life by eating Ray's food. We then duly recovered and had a game of cricket, were there was a few injured.

'Things to remember.
1. Every other day don't eat because Ray cooks it.
2. Don't play football with Ray.
3. Don't get ripped off with so called gifts, because you can get the stuff at least 20p cheaper.
4. Don't learn how to play the game of "Nations".

Mathew Beg.'

It should be noted that Ray and Jean Lawman had taken over as Wardens, Mike Brook having departed to Cambridge. To continue:

'Today's log written this evening – now! 6th June 1977.
This morning I awoke, which is obvious, to see what I thought to be the beginning of a lovely day, how wrong I was.

'After breakfast, which I cannot remember as I was still asleep. I went for a walk in the sunshine to see the Stack. On reaching the Stack it began to rain. After a few minutes, by which time Jamie, Peter and myself were completely soaked, Jamie remarked observantly, "It's going to rain".

'When I returned to the cottage and changed I sat and read a book. Lunch was unclassified stuff and baked beans, although it was very nice.

'After lunch I climbed the Knoll with my swimming costume and lay down to observe two lonely figures wandering off to find Mr Stanbury, who was apparently resting his eyes near the Razorbill hide. He was woken and persuaded to come down to the quay to observe us swimming, he's supposed to stop us drowning?

'The pioneer – me – was first in, all the 4th years went in but one, guess who, then I succeeded in cutting my foot open, then laised around all day.'

Jamie Roberts and Graham Romp.

'Tuesday June 7th 1977. Jubilee Day.
Awoke at 7.30 a.m. and stepped outside to see the island dressed overall – two flags really, all we could muster – on a clear morning

with a stiff northerly breeze. Our two flags – Heralds please note – must be described, so I beg to digress.

'The first, the Welsh flag, the "Draig Goch". The second the school flag (where on *earth* did it come from?) A horse, white, rampant on a field sable. In my best evening class Welsh this translates as, "Cefyl gwynyn y cae di" – I think! Oh this learning what a thing it is!

'Anyway this was the scene that confronted me, two flags resisting the buffets of the wind. No human beings insight, but as an early riser I am accustomed to this. A glance at the quay reassured me that Idi Amin had not yet arrived.

'After a few minutes our leader joined me at the door of the bunkhouse. Five lines of "Land of Hope and Glory" achieved more than threats or entreaties on other more normal mornings; as one the bunkhouse arose. Colin Finbow – in unkindly vein I thought – flung ten pence at us, our leader was quick to pocket it, beaming. But all were early for breakfast. Still no sign of Idi.

'Despite the breeze everyone did "their own thing" after breakfast. Light was easily sufficient for the filmers to film, it was pleasant enough for the walkers to walk and just sitters to just sit. The Warden of Aberlleferni (sic) dug a 'uge 'ole henceforth to be known as Jubilee Pit.

'In honour of the Royal occasion, lunch and dinner were reversed. A superb lunch meant that, after an hour and a half sunbathing I felt the need to retire for an hour. I maintain that I was not the only one; however I seem to be the only one to admit it. Sighted a small yacht in South Haven, but Idi not aboard.

'Five o'clock brought Jubilee Cricket match and a considerable drop in temperature. G.T.R. distinguished himself:-
a. By knocking the score along to 100 for 5.
b. Suggesting that as a superb Jubilee tea was being prepared by Ray and Jean, he was willing to shelve his Republican sympathies for the duration of the meal.

'Gin and Tonic preceded the tea and what a tea it was! Ray and Jean loaded the table with scones, buns, cakes, so much that from first to last we were defeated. A great meal and thanks from us all to our hosts, who must have spent ages preparing it all. There would have been plenty for Idi had he come.

'The evening was spent – by most adults at least – in traditional manner, sitting by the driftwood fire. Conversation is non existent; since most, like me, cannot hear what is said over the hiss of the Tilleys. Seriously it is nice to be back, I believe this is my seventh visit and it has lost none of its charm, this island.

'It's rather nice to hear the comment of Mrs C- - – (a near relative of mine) – as a person on her first visit. In any case where could

Jubilee day be better, more enjoyably spent, than on Skokholm.
   'I don't think Idi's non appearance worried us unduly.'

Tony Collier

'*Wednesday 8th June 1977, Jubilee day plus one.*
   In memory, days on Skokholm are bright and sunny. I can now
remember 270 of them and today must rank as one of the most
perfect. Hot, cloudless, a riot of flowers, a skyful of birds, good
company, better and better food – the whole thing from a sizzling
breakfast to a spitting driftwood fire makes the effort involved in
getting here more than worthwhile. But enough of the purple
passages!
   'T.C. woke early as usual (he sleeps too much during the day) and
coughed loudly outside my room, well before the required hour –
but we filled in the time watching the chickens and ducks have
their breakfast. It is difficult to say what was done during a day
which was not notable for birds, but a few incidents will give the
general flavour.
   'The film crew filmed cuckoo spit on bracken fronds, the cricket
squad played stripped to the waist, the swimmers swam briefly, the
helicopter relieved the lighthouse. The boat from Dale Fort never
came but gave us a lot of fun looking for it, several staff nearly had a
heart attack pumping the water and have started a fund for a bigger
pipe. The Headmaster emerged in shorts and Philip emerged
through his jeans, the whole party went red stroke brown, a
splendid uneventful day.
   'The pressure of all this leisure is taking its toll. Colin in the 'tonic
crisis', (we are short on tonic or high on gin, whichever way you
look at it), used whisky to dilute his gin. In fact there is a minor
crisis with the gin, following a Jubilee excess of loyal toasts and we
are reduced to only one session a day.
   'Books being read vary from "Up funnel, down Screw", to open
university holiday tasks, through "Dogs of War" and "Snotty".
Perhaps this is the place to say a little about the party.
   'The oldest (almost), brownest and baldest has been before and
never ceases telling everyone else about it. His razor has broken. He
wrote the log, he sleeps a lot.
   'The film man Colin is only little, so he has a big assistant Greg,
who carries heavy things around for him and argues with him over
the shots.
   'Our Warden John runs about a lot and spends his time in his pit.
This year he brought Elaine, otherwise he would not come.
   'The round one Tony has been before and he also would not
come without Doreen this year.

'The veterans include Jamie, who looks like a cherub but isn't. Graham, who doesn't look like a cherub and isn't. Peter, who fortunately has lost his voice and Matthew who has returned to continue his war of attrition with Ray – he lost last year.

'The new arrivals include Tony – Jumbo Jaws – Jarret and a sprinkling of cricketers, Steve and the Prof G.T.R., who can play Black Widow. Then there is Philip, whose jeans are going through a lot this week and can't play Black Widow. Mark who is the biggest incentive to the cooks since Friar Tuck and the other Tony (Peghay) who dashes about like a disturbed Oystercatcher parent.

'A large and motley bunch! The thirty fifth Forest Hill party in all its glory. Now the day is closing, darkness draweth nigh, shadows of the evening steal across the sky and we must out after Shearwaters and Stormies. We are sitting around replete after demolishing an entire tin of water biscuits and trying hard to stay awake. Conversation is at a minimum as you can't hear anything above the noise of the Tilleys.'

Dave Stanbury.

'Thursday 9th June 1997. Jubilee day plus two.
Today has been quite fertigan (fatiguing). Beginning as it did at 1.30 a.m. when myself and the old team was out at the crack of dawn watchin and a listening at the Stormy Petrels, what we never did hear and also the Shearwaters that we did. Except that one of them was a Leach's Petrel, which did sing a different tune like a woodpecker a laughin and at no time did the temperature of our bodies exceed 98.5. We then was returning after we see them when we see a you f.o. and stars in the eavons.

'Velvet swoop of boiling birds and the fresh dark sprinkled with stars and the sea just audible above the hiss of the Tilley lamp. Tingling cold as the Shearwaters gradually appeared and filled the night with waddling till we waddled home and interrupted our day with sleep.

'Suddenly the bell for breakfast and the day resumed, clear, hot and sea blue. The events of the early day seemed far away and everyone wondering if Matthew really caught a rabbit or Tony Hunter or what. Then off to the flora and the island blossoming under our scouting. A day set fair to film flowers. A coffee break – then cries and shouts of "the boat, the boat's on its way". Like the remembered relief of the delayed boat's arrival after being stormbound on my last visit. This boat was the Dale boat, Grassholm bound.

'We boarded the boat with somewhat of a tenshun in the air for the skipper, David, could not take us all on his craft and so the third years had to stop behind; at least some of them did because we was able to take the two Tonies and Phillip, who never really wanted to go (he said).

'We set out from South Haven in fair weather with the sun to windward and the smiles on our faces for David Stanbury – alias Captain Fitzroy – was drivin and I – alias Captain Birdseye – took up my place on the bulwarks, bollards, gunwhales or whatever they are called, to take pictures of the sea with a zoom lens what I did not need, since the sea came very close and we all sat quite attached to it and vice versa.

'The sea it blew a gale of wind and it was lovely – Dave said. All our feet was awash and at no time did the temperature exceed 60 degrees below. Phillip said he never really want to come anyway – I believed him. Jamie said it was so wet he didn't care and he didn't. Graham dripped from all his points and went very quiet. Dave and David the skipper and John all smiled – sometimes they grinned.

'Skokholm it took a long time to go behind us so I guessed we was not no-where near Grassholm yet. Greg hid all the cameras from the sea since his 'ands was too frozen to hold them and we was all very quiet, exceptin the skipper and Dave, who kept on talkin about food and things some of us was not very interested in. The dissapointed third years who stayed behind never knew what they was missin – lucky beggars some of us thought. We gallant seafarers was missin lunch – which was just as well in view of the state of the seas.

'Tony by this time had got on his funny hood and Doreen was makin remarks about his head, but it was very dry which is more than you say for Matthew, who had to borrow a waterproof to put over his wet clothes to prevent them gettin dry. Phillip – who never wanted to come anyway – started to suffer from exposure – perhaps due to the 'ole in his jeans and the skipper gave him a cagoule and overtrasis to keep out the draft (we had had baked beans and sossiges for breakfast).

'I lifted my head over the bows and we was suddenly at Grassholm for the sky it were full of Gannets and the rocks were white with them like flowers and in the sky they was black. They had shat all over the rocks and you could smell it, which bearin in mind the state of the sea, Elaine did not find very agreeable. Nor did some of us. Phillip never really wanted to come and by now nor did Jamie.

'The skipper took us round the island several times and we did see seals and then we went round again, which was fun and then again which was cruel, then again which was unkind and then again when Dave said he thought it was very kind and some of us did not agree.

'One by one we went to the back of the boat where it was warmer and Jamie sat in the bows and looked very peculiar – which is nothing to worry about. John he drove the boat and went in all the big waves becos he like them and so do I lest my readers should think me without sea legs. Matthew went to sleep, Tony Hunter started to shiver so he could go in the warm bit by the engine. Tony Jarrett started to look like he never really wanted to come, Doreen and Elaine looked very determined.

'The skipper gave us some beer, which was very kind but still the temperature did not exceed 60 degrees below. The beer it had a side effect on some of us, the younger members of the crew had orange squash, which also had a side effect and more us started to look determined. The sound of rushin water and cold and the drink was havin an effect on us and there was no loo on the boat. Graham he said could he pee over the side, so we held his coat while he did. Five minutes later he stopped. Some of us, especially Peter was also burstin and Doreen and Elaine looked very determined.

'John was going fast towards home when suddenly it was decided, I know not by whom, to visit Skomer and we sailed over past the Gannets or Guillemots or whatever – we didn't care by now. One intrepid birdwatcher, who shall be nameless (Peter) doubled in agony and said "sod the Guillemots, who wants to see Guillemots" and peed over the side.

'Such relief as we turned from Skomer to point homeward, when suddenly a little fishin boat we past left off a red flare and we was off to rescue it. This was too much and four of us lined up to pee over the side at once, which was somethin of a record seein the boat was not even on fire.

'We were about to save the boat (*Vera*) when the coastguard sent in the cavalry, as John put it and H.M.S. *Woodlark* steamed in like an episode of "Warship" and saved it – the *Vera*.

'It started to rain, which was not very kind. When we got back the skipper would not bring the boat into South Haven, so we had to come in in a little rubber dinghy, which was very exciting. Doreen and Elaine went first, because their need was greatest. Jean had made us a great meal as usel. It was all very fertigan, which is why I have now stopped the record of this voyage.'

Colin Finbow, with apologies to John Chapender.

'P.S. Those of us who did not take part in the "Fertigan" trip to Grassholm stayed behind to see the "velvet swoop of boiling birds and the fresh dark sprinkled with stars and the sea which was just audible over the hiss of the Tilleys". When the intrepid adventurers returned their temperature at no time exceeded 60 degrees below all evening.'

'Friday 10th June 1977.

Woke up, pissing down with rain, only one day to go before our release! Sossiges and eggs again for breakfast, all very fertigan as usual. Slave driver Stanbury conned us into "breaking the back of cleaning the bunkhouse", which we duly proceeded to do with pleasure-ish.

'Still pissing down so had to play cards in the Common room – who suggested swimming. A few fools – Peter, Mark and Phillip, who didn't want to go anyway, went bird watching of which two nameless persons – Phillip and Mark – returned late for lunch.

'After lunch we were ordered to make a gull count, during which we got wet (not only from the rain which was still pissing down) and cold and on top of this many of us had packed away our dry trousers ready for tomorrow.

'In the evening slave driver Stanbury said "who is doing the log". We pretended not to hear his voice over the hiss of the Tilleys, but we were found out, so here we are. All very fertigan.'

'Who other than schoolboys could have written such descriptive phrases – "the velvet swoop of boiling birds" – "the tingling cold' and 'the fresh dark sprinkled with stars".'

Sadly, and largely because a few tragic accidents involving school parties have been hyped up by the media, few teachers will take the risk of organising similar trips, in case they get sued because someone twists his foot in a rabbit hole. Whatever care is taken and whatever rules are formulated to avoid them, accidents will always happen. To deny children adventure means they will not recognise danger and even more tragedies will ensue.

A hard working 'model'.

80

ABOVE: Michael Betts, Sam Robins and Jean
Lawman on Crab Bay Rocks. BELOW: Can't think
why they are so tired! – Sketch by Huw Morgan.

LEFT: A bit of a swell off Mad Bay Point. RIGHT:
Smartening up Blacksmith's Landing. BELOW:
Repairing the Wheelhouse roof.

SECRET SPRINGS

Left on my own with the Wardens – Graham and Liz Gynn – after the goat catchers had departed, I learned more about their work and the importance of their observations, than I might otherwise have done if I had been a member of a larger party.

Accompanying them on their morning rounds I was shown the extent of the bird colonies and where to look for different species, especially the areas where first migrants and rarities are likely to turn up. They told me that at that time – in 1981 – it was estimated that 35,000 pairs of Manx shearwaters nested on the island. Coupled to an estimated 100,000 pairs on neighbouring Skomer, this made the two islands the principal breeding colony of these birds.

As if that were not enough it was also estimated that 6,200 pairs of storm petrels, 2,500 pairs of puffins, 4,600 pairs of lesser black back gulls and 1,250 pairs of herring gulls all nested on this little 240 acre island. To the mathematically minded this all works out at just over 200 nests to the acre. It takes no account of cliff-nesting birds such as guillemots, razorbills and fulmars. At that time these consisted of 100, 374 and 17 pairs respectively. Currently in 1997 there are more like 300 guillemots, 550 razorbills and 137 fulmars.

Due to an outbreak of botulism – caused by scavenging on mainland waste tips – the herring gull population collapsed in the 1980s, but is now showing signs of recovering. But the lesser black back gull seems to be on the decline, most probably due to shortage of food because of a change in the Fisheries Policy. This may be no bad thing because it gives the ground nesting birds such as lapwing, skylark, oystercatchers, meadow pipits and ducks a better chance. They all nest in significant numbers, but suffer severe predation from the gulls.

There are many others too numerous to mention who nest on the island, some successfully and others less fortunate. Occasionally peregrine, buzzards, ravens and even the rare chough manage to rear their young.

The importance of headlands and offshore islands to migrating birds' flight lines was explained, as was the possibility of finding a rarity that had been blown off course by severe gales. Rarities that have turned up over the years include such species as pectoral sandpiper, black headed bunting, scarlet rosefinch, Bonelli's warbler, black browed albatross and more recently a white throated robin.

These are just a few examples but there are many others and you never know when you walk out of the house in the morning what rarity may have turned up. You may see the first swallow of the season, a black redstart or a melodious warbler. At the moment (October 1997) the island list stands at 274 species. There is always the chance you will be the first to spot a new one.

Besides looking out for birds and plotting nest sites, weather observations, temperature and rainfall all had to be recorded. Then there was the insect life – butterflies, bumble bees and anything else that moved was all noted. Also numbers of seals round the island, porpoises, dolphins and even the occasional whale all had to be written down on a special form.

I became fascinated by their work and the nature of their lifestyle, but I could not help but comment on the condition of the buildings and the difficulties under which they had to work.

The water supply still came from the same well that it does today, but at that time it was open to the elements and all manner of unmentionable detritus found its way into the opening. Water was extracted by means of a hand pump and it was not unusual for ladies to wash their hair over the well, while a friend did the pumping.

For their personal washing purposes visitors were requested to use the rain water tubs around the buildings; if these were dry they had to fetch the water from the well, using a suitable container. The last task on a Saturday morning that the visitors were expected to assist in was 'the water run'. This involved filling a large tank, temporarily placed in the borrowed lighthouse dumper, from the well and bringing the contents up to the drinking water tank outside the Wheelhouse. Here a chain of persons had to be formed to bucket it up into the tank. There usually had to be several runs before the Warden was satisfied that the supply was sufficiently replenished.

The state of the buildings left a lot to be desired, the roof of the Wheelhouse was decidedly rocky and the purlins had rotted off where they butted in to the gable ends of the cottage. I was informed that the interior condition of the buildings always suffered severe deterioration through being uninhabited during the winter months, there being no-one on the island between early November and mid-March.

On their return in the spring the Wardens were always hard put to it to get everything in a tolerable state for the visitors, the first of whom usually arrived in early April. Seeing the problems involved I tentatively offered my services the following spring to assist opening the place up. This offer was seized upon with alacrity by

Graham and Liz. We collected another half dozen or so volunteers, notably Les Hall and family and Mick and Anne Brown. There were others in the early days, but those were the regular stalwarts who pioneered the first 'Work Parties'.

We quickly discovered that Skokholm in the early spring was a different place to what it was in high summer, or autumn for that matter. The cold could be intense and the buildings and bedding were slow to warm up, while a feeling of damp pervaded the air. People quickly learned not to get their clothing wet, because drying facilities were non-existent.

Some good work was done in those early days – roof repairs, interior walls re-rendered where necessary, new sinks in the Wheelhouse and new windows in the bunkhouse and cottage. Everyone worked with tremendous zest and enthusiasm and left with the feeling that we had given the Wardens a good start for the coming season.

Stephen Sutcliffe was chairman of the Islands Committee at that time and saw the potential contained in annual work parties to improve the conditions. Together we worked out a programme of repair and rebuilding of the observatory buildings, which was to occupy successive volunteer parties for the next ten years. The aim was to upgrade the standard of accommodation for both visitors and Wardens.

In 1985 Stephen resigned and was appointed Warden on Skomer. He has since moved on to other things, his quick able brain and financial flair sorely missed in Trust counsels.

The task for the spring work party of 1984 was to re-roof the Wheelhouse. The main timbers had been cracked for some time and had been spliced and shored up on a number of occasions. Even so, the whole lot was in danger of collapsing onto the diners below.

For the first landing on 6 March 1984 the Wardens arrived over an unbelievably calm sea in an overcrowded boat. It took over two hours to unload tons of timber and cement. In addition there were eight hundred slates for the roof, which were only able to be shifted as far as the crane in the time available. The dumper gave up working and much trust was placed in the elements by leaving everything just out of the sea's reach for the night.

The Wardens spent the next few days shifting slates up to the first corner of the track by wheelbarrow and the sheets of plywood and some timber by hand up to the observatory. Fortunately a mechanic was among the workmen who came over to the lighthouse on Thursday and he fixed the dumper sufficiently for us to move everything up and store it under polythene.

The weather continued calm and rainless for three weeks, enabling the Wardens to prepare for the work party and do necessary re-decoration.

'March 21st 1984.
First day of spring and the first Wheatears arrived. Not much else around though. Nettles are just showing as are the tops of bluebell leaves. No flowers yet, the island is unusually dry and I have had to rescue the old well tadpoles from a dessicating death.'

Two days later the weather had completely altered – as it has a habit of doing on offshore islands: 'Weather unspeakably vile all of a sudden – south east force nine and lashing rain. North Haven hide is half way down the gulley. The Seawatch hide has toppled from its rock in the quarry and the gull hide is in pieces.'

After a long dry spell, Sod's Law continued to apply with regard to the weather, when the time came for the work party to cross over. At that time Dale Sailing Co had their headquarters in Dale, where the loading facilities were not good. Only for an hour at about half tide could we load straight on to the boat from somebody's courtyard on the Dale Fort side of the harbour. Most often we had to transfer from shore to boat by inflatable dinghy. If there was any quantity of cargo to go over it all had to be loaded on to an ex-army amphibious DUKW, which was liable to conk out half way through the transfer. All this meant that loads had to be doubled handled on to the DUKW and then unloaded on to the *Dale Princess*. If there was anything of a sea running, which there was on this occasion, it could be quite a hazardous exercise.

To add to our troubles the conditions at South Haven were impossible and we had to use the alternative Blacksmith's Landing, in North Haven. This was before it was generally smartened up with steps and a landing platform.

Besides our personal gear and food we had a portable generator, concrete mixer, tools and sundry building materials to unload. Thanks to Campbell's superb seamanship we managed to land it all safely. By the time we had got it all unloaded we were pretty well knackered and we then had the long haul up the cliff.

The work party consisted of myself and son Charles, Les Hall and Moira, Peter Willcock, Peter Tithecott, Martin Garnett and two others.

Before we had arrived Graham and Liz had cleared everything out of the Wheelhouse and transferred the cooking and eating facilities to the laboratory. This meant we could get straight into work, which was just as well because we had only been allowed a fortnight to do the job.

After everyone had settled in and had a quick lunch, Graham took those who had not been before on a tour of the island. When they got back they found the roof of the Wheelhouse no longer there. What had happened was that Les and I had got up on top and banged around a bit and the whole lot had collapsed, though fortunately we did not go with it. The rest of the day was spent clearing old tiles and timber out of the inside. I had brought my chainsaw with me and, which would have probably apalled the purists, if they had but known, I cut the old ex-*Alice Williams* timbers up for firewood.

When we had cleared up the debris and started to look at the walls, preparatory to erecting the main roofing frames, it was abundantly clear that there was not much holding the rest of the building up. We were particularly concerned that the gable ends would fall out, especially the westernmost. We did not breathe freely until we had made up the three main frames, got them in position and braced the whole lot together with the purlins. This took us until Tuesday night – we were up to schedule, just. Wednesday was spent fixing the rafters and we made a start on the tiling battens. As we were to discover on numerous future occasions the powers that be did not have the remotest idea how to estimate the time repair jobs were likely to take and we were always working flat out into the night to get completed in time for the visitors come Saturday.

Thursday saw the last of the battens put on and we started tiling, which we did not finish until nine o'clock on the Friday night. Les Hall, who was leaving on Saturday and was the only skilled builder in the group, was up at the crack of dawn putting lead flashing round the chimney stack.

The second week was spent redecorating the Wheelhouse, building new cupboards either side of the chimney breast and generally getting everything back in to shape so that it could once more function as the kitchen-cum-dining room.

There was one unpleasant accident when Mick Brown, who came for the second week, ran a wood splinter through his hand and had to be carted off to hospital. However, he soon come back and the work was completed, the wheel put back, the *Alice Williams* nameboard and the lifebuoys all returning so that everything looked back to normal.

Summer visitors to the island frequently comment that they would like to be there 'to see what it's like in the winter gales'. Perhaps the following entry from Graham and Liz Gynn's last days as Wardens might go some way towards satisfying their curiosity:

'Our last visitors left on 11th September, since that date Liz and I have been in residence alone. The autumn in general has been very windy and today, the day we were supposed to leave is certainly no exception. There is a force nine gale and continuous rain from the south west. The Wheelhouse door blew open and the kitchen was soggy at breakfast time. The chickens are miserable and like most days this autumn the wind is too strong for any observable bird movement. Any birds on the island, like the first Dunnock of the year seen yesterday, will be firmly fixed in the densest vegetation. On a day like this the robins and wrens, that have recently been so vocal, are silent.

'This autumn has been rather disappointing as far as varieties are concerned, as a direct consequence of the windy weather. But an Ortolan Bunting and an Icterine Warbler in September was duplicated in October. A Corncrake was seen by Liz and heard by both of us on the last day of September. It is interesting to note that the behaviour of our Corncrake was no different from those recorded before. It was seen once and flew to an area of bracken and despite attempts to flush it, was not seen again.

'The gales continue today, force eight and very gloomy but no precipitation until drizzle at sunset. Still no birds – all the little jobs skulking in the flattened bracken and down rabbit holes. Seawatching also very unrewarding, ten Kittiwakes, eleven Auks and one Gannet plus a southbound flock of ten Cormorants, all in one hour.

'Graham disappeared in the Trinity House helicopter at 2p.m. leaving me to wait for the boat and have – "The boat's coming round St Anne's" panic all on my own. Main tasks in this event are to clear the Wheelhouse of current feeding utensils, catch chickens, wire up doors, pack bed, dismantle gas fittings and get all down to the landing.

'Wind west north west overnight and is now down to about five, sea is slightly choppy over a long swell. Boat is possible and met men say a big high is due over south Britain for the next three days. I'll start packing up.

'P.S. Campbell had to help catch the chickens.'

LEFT: There is much to be done when the
Wardens return. (Photo by Theresa Purcell) RIGHT
& BELOW: The Wheelhouse roof takes shape.

LEFT: Peter Tithecott. RIGHT: The late 'Kenny the Car Park' Edwards, who ruled the Martinshaven car park. BELOW: Graham and Liz Gynn, Warden 1981-84 with Anna Sutcliffe.

FIFTY NOT OUT

The Jubilee Cricket Match by Graham Gynn, Warden from 1981-1984

In 1933 a team from Marloes visited Skokholm to play cricket with a Skokholm team on the meadow in front of the farm buildings. On the weekend of 6 August 1983, the fiftieth anniversary of the match, it was planned to repeat the occasion. It was hoped that the home team would reverse the result of the previous occasion.

The appropriate entry in the log reads as follows:

'On Saturday the 6th August the *Dale Princess* brought the week's visitors, together with Steve, Anna and Peter Sutcliffe, Mick Brown and John, Helen and Charles Lewis who came over to prepare the pitch and the food.

'After a great deal of deliberation and trial and error to find a twenty two yard strip with the minimum number of rabbit holes, the wicket was set up; roughly in the middle of the meadow. Holes were filled with whatever was available, thistles were cleared from the outfield and the boundary marked with canes and lengths of driftwood and rope, which it was hoped would impede the cricket ball's progress into the bracken.

'Jean Gynn brought festoons of flags and bunting, which were hung from the lab to the cottage and back again. The dumper was rigged with flagpoles fore and aft and the scene was well and truly set for the morrow.

'A cricket practice was held that evening and Martin Garnett (Warden 1969) proved to be a ferocious bowler, but even so no-one managed to hit the wicket during two hours' play – an ill omen for the next day. John utterly failed to see the ball and elected himself groundsman.

'The next day dawned bright and glorious, perfect cricket weather. After breakfast the panic began; hundreds of sandwiches were made in rapid time. Tables were brought out and covered with paper cloths. Notices made to direct the gents to the Elsan pit, a donation box made, a table selling books set up and the beer stall erected on a table that fitted nicely over the wall by the lab.

'While all this was going on John and Charles were sweating to get the wicket ready. The rabbits had reopened the holes we had filled in the previous evening and the chickens had eaten the flour with which we had marked the crease.

91

'Come twelve o'clock and all looked "regular jamboree" as the boat rounded the Deer Park, packed to the hilt with figures. The tide was unfortunately at its lowest and Marloes cricket team, their gear, Marloes villagers with ample picnics, B.B.C. Wales and their cameras all had to climb over the seaweed covered rocks beyond the quay in South Haven.

'It was successfully managed though and after a brief talk on Shearwater burrows, and the fire danger the first boatload walked up to the Home Meadow to the whirring of T.V. cameras.

'Two more boatloads arrived, some 150 people in total including David Saunders and family, Eileen Williams, Mike Alexander and his Skomer army, Jack Donovan, Graham Rees, Roscoe Howells, John Barratt, Kenny Edwards, the Martinshaven car park man, who looked very smart in knotted handkerchief, many Marloes villagers and ex-Warden Peter Davis and wife, who hadn't been back to Skokholm since the 1950s.

'The cricket match started after the second boat arrived, Marloes won the toss and elected to bat. They looked splendid dressed in their whites and our team looked less professional but sort of multi-coloured.

'Eileen Williams – trust booking officer – was appointed scorer and Mr Sutcliffe senior, umpire. Stephen Sutcliffe, as chairman of the committee, assumed captainship and opened the bowling from the well end. Fired by the occasion he took the first wicket in the first over. What a surprise, but more was to follow, Martin took a wicket in the second over and Steve took a third in the third over. What was going on we were doing well.

'Marloes then began to settle down and made a few runs, but the wickets kept falling. It wasn't until their captain, Peter Turvey – a Trust member playing for the opposition – entered the lists and stiffened their ranks that fours and sixes were made with rather too much regularity. Two more wickets fell and then B. Richards batted. Between the two seventy four runs were scored which gave the home team a mammoth task. Eventually R. Turvey was caught spectacularly by Peter Sutcliffe and their last man dismissed soon afterwards.

'The island team had managed, much to our surprise, to get their entire team out within the allotted twenty five overs and Stephen Sutcliffe, David Little and Martin Garnett proved effective bowlers.

'After a long break for beer, sandwiches, chat and relaxing in the glorious sunshine, the match resumed. Peter Sutcliffe faced the bowling first. He scored one run but managed to scare the bowlers into giving us a few wides.

92

'Mike Brook hit a four and made a couple of singles before being run out much to his annoyance and ours too, for we were expecting great things from the ex-warden and efficient wicket keeper.

'Martin Garnett fell prematurely to a bad bounce and Stephen Sutcliffe after hitting out well, hit one straight at the bowler and was duly caught. Stephen Redpath, who plays for Dyfed Colts was out for a duck and I was ignominiously dismissed first ball, which ran along the ground under my bat and sent the stumps flying – all recorded on T.V.

'The trilogy of ducks was completed by Andy Gillham and so it was left to David Little and Campbell Reynolds to make the runs. They did very well but eventually David fell l.b.w. and the inexperienced Mick – "how do I hold the bat" – Brown didn't last long. Our last man was Bill Arnold from the lighthouse and he made two before Campbell was out for 18. So we were all out for 67; yes, we lost, but did so with far more panache than expected.

'The teams.

Marloes		Skokholm	
T. Howell	0	Peter Sutcliffe	1
S. Bowen	8	Mike Brook	6
T. Sturley	1	David Little	21
D. Regan	9	Martin Garnett	5
J. Howell	0	Stephen Sutcliffe	4
B. Stephens	5	Stephen Redpath	0
P. Turvey	41	Graham Gynn	0
R. Scale	13	Andy Gillham	0
P. Griffiths	0	Campbell Reynolds	18
B. Richards	33	Mick Brown	0
A. Sturley	0	Bill Arnold	2
	127		62

'At the end of the game Stephen Sutcliffe thanked everybody and also presented David Stanbury, our most regular visitor, with a framed memorial of five photographs commemorating the island's fifty years of bird observations.

'The clear up operation, supervised by Mike Alexander, then proceeded as the *Dale Princess* – helmed by George Sturley – took the hordes away and by early evening all was back to normal.

'Two days later all the peat used to fill the holes in the wicket was scattered and the rabbits had also eaten the flour that marked the crease. Not a trace of the day remains, the visitors did little damage to the reserve and the drought ridden vegetation stood up well to perhaps the biggest invasion Skokholm had ever witnessed.'

ABOVE: Jack and Jean Donovan. BELOW: 1983 cricket team l to r back row: Mike Brooke, Graham Gynn, Steve Sutcliffe, Steve Redpath, Peter Sutcliffe, Mick Brown; front row: David Little, Bill Arnold, Andy Gillingham, Campbell Reynolds, Martin Garnett.

ABOVE: The cricket match of 1983. BELOW: The
boat arrives at the end of the week.

ABOVE: A bit of a blow in South Haven. BELOW:
Another view of the cottage.

96

ROUGH AND TOUGH

Graham and Liz Gynn left at the end of 1984 after four years as Wardens. Rob Wolstenholme and Amanda Holman were appointed to take their places. As is usual Rob and Amanda had gone over in early March but had to be evacuated after only a few days because Amanda became affected by a virus infection. Happily she quickly recovered and it was agreed that they would return with the work party the first week in April.

The work party consisted of Stephen and Ian Sutcliffe, Mick and Anne Brown and Helen and myself. Stephen at that time was chairman of the islands management committee and no doubt felt he had a responsibility to get them started.

We had just about the worst landing I have ever experienced. Wet and rough, the *Princess* could not come right in and we had to transfer by dinghy. Rob, as befitted his position as Warden, was the first to leap ashore and I went next. Judging the right moment as the dinghy was at the top of a swell I leaped for the rocks. Unfortunately I could not get a grip to pull myself up and had to yell for Rob. After what seemed an interminable wait during which I was getting very wet, he managed to reach down and grab me by the scruff and haul me up.

To make things easier we fixed a line to the dinghy so that I could pull it to shore and Campbell could drag it back to the *Princess*. Stephen meanwhile was having a free ride in the dinghy, which was alternately standing on its bow or stern with every third or fourth wave.

We got Mick transferred to the shore and unloading commenced and what a lot there was. Two bags of cement went over the side to the bottom of South Haven, as did a case of dried milk powder. Within a few minutes the whole of South Haven appeared to be covered in milk, washing all over us and everything until all our baggage and ourselves were covered in a sticky mess. If oil calms troubled waters milk most certainly does not.

All this time I was stuck on the quay upper step, hauling the dinghy from the *Princess* and holding it while the others unloaded. While all this was going on I was getting steadily wetter and wetter and Campbell was sitting up in the *Princess* laughing his head off at our antics. When we eventually got everything transferred I discovered I had put my back out and was in agony for the rest of the week.

97

While the others were sorting themselves out and finishing landing the stores I went up to the observatory to fetch the dumper. Stephen takes up the story as follows:

'John went to fetch the dumper, found that the brakes didn't work and charged the stop wall at the landing. Having set the precedent he did the trip a second time, the brakes still didn't work.'

Soon after landing and having been suitably refreshed we were soon hard at work – the landing had been recreation. The more we investigated the more we found to do. The cottage was in a mess, windows broken and plaster coming off the walls. Helen and Anne soon got down to cleaning and painting, Stephen kept hacking plaster off the walls – with great glee – and I had the job of covering up his mess with fresh plaster. I had never done any plastering before so I learned something on that trip.

Outside, the Wheelhouse roof had to be painted, a cold frame erected and the cracks in the quay filled in. A force nine gave the the Wheelhouse roof a mottled look, the cold frame blew away and the sea washed the new cement out of the quay. Not to be disheartened, Mick rebuilt the cold frame and the other two jobs we left for the new Wardens.

The other job that was most urgent was the overhaul of the brakes of the dumper. Everything was seized up solid and we had few tools. After making sundry minor adjustments with the aid of the sledgehammer, cold chisel and much bad language the dumper was given its MOT certificate.

Gradually things started to come together and we turned a damp, dirty, almost derelict farmhouse into a spruce, cosy, well-aired homely cottage. Our week was not without discomfort for, in order to sit down for the bird count with the Warden in the evenings, our chair seats were set to steam for a few hours before a constant fire attended by Helen. Every day we hauled all the mattresses and rugs out to be aired in the sun.

'Not much to be done' said Stephen at the beginning of the week – not much but work! Helen and Anne set about scrubbing floors, Amanda set about the catering while Rob wondered where to start. The wind freshened daily and was blowing a full gale on Friday and Saturday, gusting force ten at times. Stephen and I tackled the roofs and Ian cleaned out the water tanks.

High seas crashed around the coastline on Saturday. The strong gale whipped up spindrift and giant tankers battled against the waves, making their way out of Milford Haven. Not surprisingly no sign of Campbell!

The wind moderated on Sunday and we packed up slowly and then the gale and heavy seas picked up again, leaving us all uncomplainingly Skokbound. David Emmerson passed in his toy lifeboat and someone suggested calling him up on the radio for a lift to Dale, but no-one seconded the motion.

A mysterious raptor was seen around the buildings and was variously identified as a sparrowperegrine (juvenile), goshawk – lanner – saker falcon. A long debate, and poring over all the bird books in the library that evening, finally identified it as a juvenile *falco peregrinus*.

So we passed the time waiting for the boat, doing various small jobs with one eye and keeping the other on St Anne's Head for a sign of Campbell. Amanda baked banana bread and Anne made Christmas pudding – so it was back to the common room and let the world go round without us.

Russ Spencley props up the old Crab Bay hide.

ABOVE: Sam Robins and Russ Spencley work on
the North Pond hide. BELOW: Sue Barclay and
Michael Betts anxiously await new arrivals.

PRINCIPALS

After a two year stay Rob and Amanda departed after doing some useful work on the island, most notably the installation of the water ram, thus making the Saturday water run unnecessary. They recorded some unusual birds, most notably a buff breasted sandpiper and two pectoral sandpipers. They just missed a ring necked duck, a first female Pembroke record, seen by Steve Sutcliffe on an autumn visit, after they had left.

Michael Betts and Sue Barclay were appointed from a strong list of candidates. Not having met them before I suggested that they call in to see us, when passing, so that I could get to know them before turning up with the work party.

Unfortunately we got in a muddle over the time we were to meet and Helen and I were out when they arrived. After hanging around waiting for us they decided they could wait no longer and drove out of our drive just as we returned. Seeing a large van loaded to the gunwhales, driven by some strange individuals leaving the house, we thought we had been burgled and let them know it.

Explanations in a frosty atmosphere revealed that this was Michael and Sue. Happily the misunderstanding was quickly resolved and within a few minutes we were having a good laugh over a cup of coffee.

This inauspicious beginning certainly proved the saying that if you want to make a good friend start off by having a row with them. We clicked straightaway and began a wonderful nine year relationship, during which we were able to do some good work on Skokholm together.

Apart from wanting to get to know Mike and Sue, I was anxious to give them some instruction on my dumper, which was identical to the Skokholm vehicle. I felt this to be essential if, as had been the custom with previous Wardens, they were dumped down on the landing and left to their own devices. After explaining the basics I put Mike in the driving seat and he promptly drove into a wall, much to Sue's amusement.

Skokholm old timers will remember that the Warden's quarters used to be situated in the Central Block, between what used to be the toolshed and the laboratory. The accommodation was little better than a superior, no not superior, just a henhouse. It consisted of a bedroom and a squitty little office with a large window and everything open to public view. They had no privacy whatsoever, it was not all that weatherproof and how they were to be expected to give their best under those conditions passed my comprehension.

Mike and Sue echoed the comments of previous Wardens, supported by regular visitors and Work Party leaders that something must be done to improve the accommodation provided, otherwise the rapid turnover of Wardens would continue.

The agreed plan was that the bunkhouse should be turned into the Warden's quarters. This meant that they would be near the Wheelhouse and cooking facilities. The accommodation would be more roomy and they would have greater privacy.

The Central Block was to be enlarged to provide three double cabins, the laboratory would stay and the east end would house a single and a double room. For the time being the workshop would remain. Later, of course, it was converted to a double cabin now known as the Bull Pen. This perpetuated its name in Lockley's time.

We had two work parties that year. Graham Gynn came on the first one in the spring and was able to set Mike and Sue on the right tracks. We did the usual tasks, generally smartening the place up and getting ready for the coming season.

To make a happy change the management agreed to our making a start on the Central Block by doing the concrete block work in August, during a slack week. The walls could then harden off during the winter and the job be completed the following spring.

It so happened that I was on Skomer during the first week of June, helping with the gull count. Stephen Sutcliffe had become Skomer Warden the year before and Mike and Sue were appointed to Skokholm. I managed to persuade Stephen to run me over to Skokholm in his inflatable – a most exhilarating ride but well worth the bumps and wetting to see the place again. Mike and Sue seemed pleased to see us and I was able to mark out where the new foundations were to go and estimate the materials required.

August 1987 found me back on Skokholm with my son David, Russ Spencley and Paul Glendell – to build the new front wall of the Central Block. Sadly we found on arrival that Mike was in hospital with a severe throat infection; thankfully he responded to treatment and returned after a couple of days.

The concrete blocks had been delivered by helicopter, courtesy RAF Brawdy, a few days previously. Thank heaven we did not have to transfer them on the boat.

We were pleased to find that Huw Morgan, who had been over as assistant warden for the summer, had dug out the footings, so we could go straight into the building work. Poor chap – he had had quite a tough job and had come across some big boulders, probably footings of a previous building, which he had to haul out with the dumper.

It did not take us long to get the new footings in and the new corners set up and the rest of the job was plain sailing. Everybody worked well, we had a bit of time on hand so Paul, who had brought his inflatable dinghy over, took Mike and myself on a circumnavigation of the island to count guillemots and fulmar chicks. Many of the nest sites and ledges are only visible from the sea.

It was a lovely day with a gentle swell but we had not gone very far before I realised that Paul's dinghy was far from being A1 at Lloyds. We got round the Neck and Hard Point alright and up the Mad Bay side we were too busy counting nests to pay too much attention to our conveyance. I do not know how Mike felt but I was apprehensive as we rounded the Lighthouse; Paul's engine did not seem to have sufficient poke to push us along and I saw us finishing up on Grassholm or places further west. There was quite a fair swell against the rocks on the south coast and I did not fancy our chances, if we had to make a forced landing. After what seemed an age we reached Crab Bay and from then on it was relatively plain sailing.

The spring work party was to be of two weeks' duration. The Trust management, with normal parsimony expecting us to do two weeks' work in one, reluctantly agreed that we would be pushed to do it in a week. Helen and I travelled down with Paul Glendell and stopped with Mick and Anne Brown in Tenby on the Friday night, as we were to make an early start on the Saturday.

On the Saturday morning we were in Dale by 10 am in low cloud and wet rain. We met Russ Spencley and Sam Robins, who were gloomy because John Reynolds said it was too rough to go. So we sat in the Griffin and hoped it would calm down in the afternoon. Of the rest of our gang, one did not turn up, one turned up and said he could not come, but the other, who had better be nameless, professed himself willing to go.

Come 2.30, after exhausting the Griffin's hospitality, we called it off for the day and agreed to meet at 8.30 the following morning. We all went back to Tenby and camped on Mick and Anne's sitting room floor – they were not surprised to see us.

Up at 6.30 next morning and down to Dale by 8.30 am. The place was locked up but presently Campbell arrived to say that John was on his way from Neyland with the *Dale Princess*. We got all the gear and food down to Dale steps on the right of the harbour, the boat arrived and we started loading. The nameless member of our party had still not arrived, the tide was dropping fast and Campbell was anxious to get going to catch the tide on Skokholm. I could do no more than give the assent to leave, faced with the biggest job yet undertaken and three short.

103

It was a rough ride out but the sea subsided and we had quite a reasonable landing on Skokholm. Poor Sue nearly had hysterics when she saw how few of us there were to do the job in hand. She had visions of a full party of visitors a fortnight hence and nowhere to put them. Otherwise they were pleased to see us, having been on their own for a month.

Usual scramble getting gear up from the harbour; the buildings had wintered well and my blockwork of the previous August was still standing. Because we were short of help and had lost a day I was not too popular when I suggested we get stuck straight into work, but that they did.

My diary entries for the next few days:
21st March 1988.
    'Gorgeous day today, up at 8 a.m. and saw 114 Oystercatchers by harbour.

    'Got on well with the Central Block, Russ, Sam and Paul got on with demolishing the west end and started concreting the floor, while I made up the roof trusses and the door frames.

    'A Sea King arrived from Brawdy with a ton of cement and a bag of Muesli. Unfortunately they dropped it a bit heavy, the Muesli bag burst and got mixed in with the cement. We found that the Muesli made good cement but that the cement made a poor breakfast.

    'We were lucky in that RAF Brawdy were happy to deliver heavy goods for us by fitting deliveries into their training exercises. It was done on the understanding that, if an emergency arose while they were making a delivery, the cargo, which was slung in a net beneath the helicopter would have to be dumped, most probably in the sea.'

25th March 1988 extract from my diary:
    'Had three busy days working on cabins fighting against force nine winds. Paul and Sam put up the divisions between the cabins while Russ and I managed to get the roofing sheets on during the occasional lulls in the wind. I got the three of them helping put the south facing sheets on this morning after breakfast, because of a forecast force nine, hail and rain showers imminent. We got them on by coffee time and I gave the boys the rest of the morning off. As it turned out we need not have panicked because the rest of the morning was quite pleasant, sunny and wind not too strong. But in the afternoon the wind got up giving terrific seas and heavy rain.

    'Spoke to son David on the radio; because of the shortage of help he agreed to come over next week. Huw and Renate are also supposed to be coming and possibly one or two from Manpower

Services. Mike is wondering about having Manpower Services on a regular basis, but I would not be happy mixing them with Work Party Volunteers. I think and hope I managed to put him off the idea.

'Went for a walk with Helen this evening and watched the high seas in Crab Bay. John Reynolds talks about coming over tomorrow afternoon but I don't see it happening unless the sea drops considerably. We have been expecting him all week with cargo, but it has been much too rough.

'The boys have been out this evening and have seen a wader they cannot identify. The nearest they can come up with is a little stint. At the moment they are arguing it out with reference books.'

26th March 1988
'Russ and Sam kept getting fleeting glimpses of the wader they cannot identify; most annoying.

'The generator conked out yesterday. We stripped it down and found a coked up valve. No valve lifter so we rubbed the face with an emery cloth – *in situ* – put it together and it went. Today it was charging the battery for the radio when there was a nasty noise and it conked again. The oil had all drained out of the crankcase and it had seized up solid.

'Sue radioed Campbell to bring us a replacement generator but the battery gave out half way through the conversation. So fingers crossed that the message got through. It is pretty important that we have a replacement because if I cannot run my power saw and other tools we will be up the creek.

'Quite rough but bright day; we wondered if the boat would come. We had almost given up hope when we saw it round St Anne's head at about 6 p.m. Usual scramble down to South Haven, boat making heavy weather and spray going right over. It eventually made it, fond farewells to Helen, Russ, Sam and Paul and some surplus hens which we are taking back to Copse Green. We were sad to see them all go; we were a happy crowd and got some good work done.'

27th March 1988
'Very quiet without Helen and the others but David, Huw and Renate have settled in well. Huw has been lining the roofs of the cabins and David and myself extending the roof of the lab. Renate has been painting the doors and frames.

'Lovely sunny day, a bit fresh but not unpleasant, quiet day for birds, 37 oystercatchers, a woodpigeon, a rook and ragged winged buzzard.'

105

29th March 1988

'Rod Billen turned up yesterday; he is a professional plasterer and it has not taken him long to give our building efforts a fresh look. He has a crafty way of putting plaster on a concrete block wall in such a manner that it looks as though the wall has been built of rough stone. This gives it a very effective look, quite in keeping with the rest of the buildings.

'The wind dropped sufficiently for Stephen, Anna, Ian and Benjamin to come over in the inflatable from Skomer to bring Ian Clowes the Assistant Skomer Warden to help us out. I was able to put him on glazing the new cabin and lab windows.

'Being a full team in sight of the end of the job I was able to let David have a go at the old lighthouse dumper, which was in a most obstreperous mood. Mike was quite keen to have an accident with it, over a cliff!'

31st March 1988

'The cabins and lab are finished, painted, washbasins installed and the place looks like a continental holiday resort, except that it's tipping down with rain. The cabins are named Port, Bosun and Starboard, in keeping with the nautical flavour of the names of the cottage rooms. With a coat of light covered paint inside they are quite attractive and waiting for tomorrow's visitors.'

On 24 June 1988, in response to a previous invitation, His Royal Highness the Prince of Wales decided to visit this far-flung corner of his Principality.

Preparations for the visit began several days in advance, when sundry Royal secretaries and ADCs came to look the island over and agree a programme with the Trust officers. The day itself began bright and early, before breakfast, with the arrival of the security division. Everybody was told how they were expected to behave. A security check was made and one or two individuals, who in the past had been somewhat vociferous in expressing Republican sympathies, were told that their youthful peccadilloes had not been forgotten. It was suggested that if they could not behave it might be a good idea if they went and watched the waves at the lighthouse, for the duration of the visit.

Next came the Trust officers, Lord Lieutenant, the Press Corps and various dignitaries who were to be presented to the Prince. Promptly at 11 am a large red helicopter of The Queen's Flight touched down on the meadow, which had been immaculately trimmed by the rabbits.

After a welcome by Mr David Mansel Lewis, President of the Trust and Lord Lieutenant of Pembrokeshire, the Prince was presented to Jack Donovan, Michael Betts, David Saunders and Ronald Lockley.

Jack Donovan and Michael Betts then accompanied him over to Mad Bay, where he enjoyed good views of razorbills, guillemots and puffins. On his return to the buildings he showed great interest in the history and development of the island. He also expressed wonderment at the island transport, the ancient dumper and took note of the forthright comments about its condition and reliability expressed by Susan Barclay.

The visit concluded, the Prince departed for Grassholm in the Royal Corps of Transport vessel *Michael Murphy V.C.* He was accompanied by Ian Prest, director of RSPB and David Saunders, the Hon Warden of Grassholm. The other Trust officers and dignitaries left for Skomer in the *Dale Princess*, so as to be ready to welcome the Prince to that island, on his return from Grassholm.

Altogether it was a most successful visit. The weather had been perfect, the birds co-operated magnificently, the Republicans kept their sympathies hidden – and we got a new dumper.

The Prince had suggested to Messrs Thwaites that we had a museum piece of a dumper that was on its last legs. A few days later a brand new dumper, a gift from Messrs Thwaites, was delivered by RAF Brawdy. The old one was whisked away, I understand to Thwaites museum, where great wonderment was expressed that it still worked.

Rebuilding the Central Block.

107

The Central Block progresses.

ABOVE: The Central Block completed. BELOW: A
dinghy trip.

LEFT: Michael Betts, Warden 1987-1995. RIGHT: Huw Morgan – sometime Assistant Warden, who drew BELOW: The mystery of the lost 'No Landing sign' solved.

ABOVE: 'The Benbo Boys': Bill, Barry, Sam and Ian. BELOW: Barry Beeley, Rod Billen and Sam Robins.

ABOVE: HRH The Prince of Wales visited
Skokholm in 1988 and is accompanied by Jack
Donovan and Michael Betts. BELOW: The Prince
talks to Sue Barclay and Ronald Lockley. (Photos
South West News)

112

RULES AND REGULATIONS

The 1990s saw a sudden proliferation of rules and regulations applicable to catering and residential establishments. Placed as we are three miles from the mainland and difficult to reach, it would have been so easy to ignore the various requirements of the Health and Safety regulations. Rather than risk a visit from the Inspectorate in mid-season and the imposition of an immediate closure order, we decided we must bring our facilities up to scratch.

The principal problem was that the cooking and washing up facilities, alongside visitors eating at table in the Wheelhouse, all on an unwashable flagstone floor with dirt interstices, simply would not do. It was no good saying that no-one had ever complained or that people preferred the homely atmosphere thus generated. One look at the cooking stoves backing on to an uneven limewashed wall – well, however did people survive under those conditions? Especially when you consider that their diet consisted of salmonella-ridden gulls' eggs, roughly slaughtered and dressed sheep – no doubt riddled with E.Coli – questionable sea beet and even more doubtful fungi.

Rather than wait for trouble either in the form of a severe outbreak of food poisoning which, according to the pundits, was long overdue, or what might prove even more dangerous, a visit by a hygiene Inspector, it was decided that the 1991 spring work party's main task would be to build a completely new kitchen.

Fire precaution regulations also gave us some cause for concern and complying with both these lots of requirements meant that large alterations and additions had to be made. This was to occupy successive work parties for the next four years.

The 1991 spring work party did not get off to a good start. Because we were going over somewhat earlier than usual, the boat was leaving from the boatyard at Neyland rather than the more usual Martinshaven. I arrived at the appointed hour on a grey and miserable day to find Campbell and John Reynolds looking at the propeller of the *Dale Princess*, which was high and dry on the quay. Jim and Annie Poole, Rod Billen, Scratch, Al, Wesley and myself all stood around feeling cold and miserable waiting to load the boat. This was difficult because they had all the hatch covers off.

Eventually they got the prop fixed to their satisfaction, slings were placed around the hull and the *Princess* was lifted by crane into the water. A brief test run down Milford Haven, then it was 'all aboard' and we were off.   113

With a dull and murky run down Milford Haven, we assumed the Reynolds knew where they were going in the mist but, when we skimmed the rocks of Thorn Island, we did rather wonder. The mists cleared as we rounded St Anne's Head and the familiar islands hove into sight, the odd puffin flew out to greet us and a skein of cormorants skimmed the waves.

Sadly only Michael was there to greet us. Sue had been taken ill the previous Monday and evacuated to hospital; we were all worried about her. This situation highlighted one of the difficulties the Wardens have to face. Having no convenient mainland base and the impossibility of getting a doctor to visit, it means they either sweat it out, get a doctor to diagnose over the radio and wait for the next boat to bring the medicine, or go to hospital. There have been occasions when it has been necessary to evacuate someone in the middle of the night. When this has happened in the past, RAF helicopters from Brawdy have air-lifted the patient straight to hospital. Probably they have done this more quickly than calling an ambulance on the mainland. Happily this situation rarely occurs, but when it does we are grateful for the swift action of the RAF.

In Sue's absence Michael manfully strove with the cooking but, after the first breakfast, Annie took over.

The present-day kitchen and larder occupy an area which used to comprise a larder and the Warden's office. Going back still further, the Warden's office used to be accommodation for the assistant cook and the Warden had his office in his personal accommodation. My diary for the next few days reads as follows:

27th and 28th March 1991
'We have built a block wall between the new larder and the kitchen. It was a flimsy stud partition before. A hole has been banged through the north wall to accommodate a six foot window over the sink. The shelving, where the plates were stacked in the Wheelhouse, has been taken out to make room for the serving hatch.

'Two very exhausting days but we have broken the back of the work. Bit dicey making a hole for the serving hatch, stones falling around our ears when we took the original beams out and cracks starting to appear in the gable end. However we wopped the new beams in quickly and it is all standing.

'600 razorbills, 100 plus puffins and guillemots today. Two peregrine and a merlin and I saw the first two woodpigeons of the year this evening. Odd how birds that are commonplace at home cause great excitement when they turn up here.'

114

30th March 1991
'Two busy days, lovely warm weather, shirt sleeves, amazing for the time of year. Dead calm today. We worked on the kitchen yesterday and started to raise the lintel over the Wheelhouse door, so that people no longer bang their heads. Fortunately managed this without the wall giving way. Amazing the Wheelhouse still stands after the way we have pulled it around the last few years.
'Changeover day today; Rod and his three lads departed. Brian Beeley, Bill Hynes, Ian Tugwell, Ray Podmore, Huw Morgan, Sharon Morris, Scratch, Al and Sam Robins arrived.
'Nearly full complement of auks around on the ledges.
'Mike went off to see Sue yesterday, leaving me in charge of the island! Absolutely petrified in case someone had an accident and I had to do a 'Mayday' on the radio. Not something you can very well practice. He found Sue much better and responding to treatment. Hope to see her back soon, we miss her very much but Annie and Sharon are feeding us very well.'

31st March 1991
'Sea Mist over everything most of the day, visibility down to about a hundred yards. I went for an early morning walk and managed to get properly lost in the fog. Thought as I left North Pond I would walk over to South Bog, instead of which I found I was about to walk over the cliff at Purple Cove. I then had the wits to do what I should have done in the first place and keep the sound of the foghorn on my right. Doing this I eventually got to "the cutting" having put up three snipe and four widgeon on the way.
'The mist cleared in the evening and Richard Humpidge came over from Skomer to see that we were not slacking and to bring us some Unibond. He also brought a Vodaphone so Michael can ring the hospital. When he tried it out we were informed Sue was much better and should be back mid-week.'

1st April 1991
'Grey blustery day; for this reason the work, mostly in the Wheelhouse, continued apace. We saw a merlin perched on the garden wall, we also had a pair of peregrine, four mallard and 127 oystercatchers. It's a dark grey night and the shearwaters are coming in well and are noisy.
'Leaving the buildings on a moonless night you are forcibly reminded of the extent of night sky, light pollution on the mainland. Not only is it difficult to find your way round when the sky is overcast, but on a clear night the stars are a breathtaking sight. The Milky Way, satellites and meteorites are a never ending source of wonderment.'

115

3rd April 1991

'Very wet and rough, seas breaking over the derrick in South Haven and washing well up the track. Devil's Teeth submerged …

'Today we moved the cooker into the new kitchen in time for lunch. This has completely altered the procedure for meals. We sort of queue up at the serving hatch and carry our food to the table. It means the Wardens are at the wrong end of the table, it's all very different to what we have been used to and the Wheelhouse is degrees colder. Glorious evening with good light for photographing waves in Mad Bay. Thirty-two meadow pipits behind the Wheelhouse this afternoon.'

4th April 1991

'Decorating Wheelhouse today, removing old sinks, makes the building look bare. Gales blowing all day and terrific seas running, spume blowing right across the island. Wind and sea took out what I thought might be a peregrine's nest in Peter's Bay. Stephen Sutcliffe was supposed to fetch me off today in the inflatable, but not a hope.

'Another depression is coming up and I would think there must be some doubt about Saturday.'

5th April 1991

'Woke to a terrific gale. Walked down to South Haven and had a record count of 163 oystercatchers. The poor beggars were sheltering down puffin burrows and anywhere they could hide from the fierce wind. Went over to Mad Bay after breakfast and had difficulty walking against the wind; … (at) times I was forced to stop and wait for a lull….

'The wind dropped in the afternoon and RAF Brawdy brought Sue back. She looks pale and obviously still weak, but morale took a definite upturn. She approves of the new kitchen arrangements.

'The main work party tasks having been completed, everybody busied themselves doing some pet project they feel would benefit the island. The spirit of enthusiasm and dedication which everyone puts in, to whatever they are doing, is wonderfully uplifting.

'Great party this evening; Michael brought the bottles out at supper time to celebrate Sue's return and my birthday – a double celebration. It's been a vintage work party; wonder if the weather will let us get off tomorrow.

'It did let us get off – just; the only time I knew Campbell to misjudge the state of the sea. The wind veered to the south east and blew into the Haven so that the transfer had to take place by dinghy

116

on a six foot swell. Some of the visitors coming in were of a decidedly green hue. It was tipping down with rain and they had inadequate wet weather gear, I felt sorry for them. But then that is one of the hazards that you have to be prepared for when visiting the island.'

LEFT: Ken Gainford at the wheel of the *Dale Princess*. RIGHT: Jack Rogers, Anna and Steve Sutcliffe putting up the rabbit exclosure. BELOW: Sarah, Sue and Helen inaugurate the new kitchen.

ABOVE: Delivery of building materials by RAF
Brawdy. BELOW: Preparing for a more orthodox
delivery by the *Dale Princess*.

ABOVE: Work party members, back row: Maurice Morgan, author, Wilf ?, Barry Beeley, Ian Tugwell, Denby Vaughan, Roz Gordon; seated: Ray Saunders, Theresa Purcell, Graham Thompson, Norman Hawkins, Sam Robins, Huw Morgan, Linda Vaughan. BELOW: Sam Robins and author contemplate a dumper ride.

119

Everything has to stop when a rare bird is
reported – sketch by Huw Morgan.

THE WORKING PARTY

Mike's meticulous approach to recording bird sightings and the pains he took to produce accurate records were a model to all observers. I was over for a weekend later on in the year and wandering up to North Pond. One evening I saw a tufted duck. I casually mentioned this when I got back to the buildings and never saw a chap so quickly galvanised into action. Apparently it was only the eleventh island sighting. Typically, Mike agonised for a good half hour as to whether it was a sub-species and I think was rather disappointed to have to decide that it was not.

So we continued the good work to improve the accommodation and facilities during the next four years, sometimes with complications, as when we built the wall of the office block in the wrong place and had to move it twelve inches to the east, or when gales north, east and southerly met over the island, bringing terrific seas.

On another occasion, when we were due to start the workshop block, gales blew for a week and we had to cancel the work party. Because the additional accommodation was urgently required we had a series of weekend work parties to get the work done.

Once the spring work party co-incided with an abnormally low spring tide, it was so low that we were able to walk over to Crab Bay rocks. This was a most eerie experience. Looked at from the Crab Bay cliff top, they do not seem much, especially when they are practically submerged under a high sea. But looked at from the sea bed they tower up and appear dark and threatening. I felt conscious of where I was and half expected the sea to come rushing back in and fill the Channel.

Mike and one or two others, much more knowledgeable than I, were going into raptures on the crustacea and minute life forms they were finding in the rock pools. I was sufficiently satisfied to climb to the top and sing 'I'm the King of the Castle' and admire the unusual view of Crab Bay.

Another first was an expedition to The Stack. Climbing down to the narrow divide that separates The Stack from the main island was the hardest part and we were glad of the ladder – necessary to bridge the gap – to get down the larger steps.

Even though it was low tide and relatively calm there was quite a strong current running through the channel. I had been told that it was possible to get across to The Stack, but you could not get back without a plank or ladder, because the step up was too big to surmount. It seemed to me that it would be a risky undertaking to launch yourself into the water and try to climb the other side.

Anyway Mike, Huw Morgan and I bridged the gap with the ladder and crawled across.

There are two ways to reach the top of The Stack. The obvious way is to turn to the left immediately on crossing and climb a near vertical cliff face. The less obvious way is to go right and, after turning a corner, a gentle slope leads to the summit. Because we did not make a proper recce we went up the hard way; at any rate it had the advantage of giving us a greater sense of achievement.

On the way up I picked up a stone and added it to the cairn on the top, thus fulfiling the vow I had made some fifteen years previously, when I made my first visit.

I have lost count of the number of work parties I have been privileged to lead on this unique island. I say privileged because it has been a privilege to lead a dedicated band, who have many times worked far into the night to get a job finished in time for the Saturday boat. I remember one Saturday morning we were all slapping plaster on the wall with one eye, while keeping the other eye cocked towards Jack Sound, hoping we would finish before the boat arrived.

We come from all walks of life and I cannot remember anyone showing a rough edge that did not fit in. Visitors to the island say we must be workaholics, which may be so, but it is only because we have discovered the joy of labour through the camaraderie of a job well done together. It is one of the tragedies of life that so many people find their work unrewarding and their efforts unappreciated. Yes, we work hard and our reward is the company of each other, good food and a job well done. But it should not be thought that we do nothing but work; it just wants the gulls to suddenly take off with a great commotion and we are all out sweeping the sky with our binoculars to determine the cause of the disturbance. It might be a buzzard, a short eared owl, a harrier or a peregrine. All the time we are keeping our eyes open to see what's about. The more ardent ones have usually quartered the island before breakfast in the hope of spotting a rarity. Coffee breaks, lunch breaks and tea breaks are all fully utilised in the hope of being able to see the first arrival of a migrant.

The following entries in the Chatty Log just about sum up the spirit in which work parties are undertaken. Firstly Jean Lawman:

'Ten years since leaving, five years since visiting and still there's nowhere to compare with Skokholm, even after a lot of travelling. My return visit this time I've enjoyed as much, if not more than ever. Very little changes and the improvements that have been made are for the better. I do miss pumping the water though.

'Wandering round the island being familiar with all its moods and secrets is once gain totally satisfying and has done much to replenish my spirits – from time to time tainted with the horrors of over civilisation on the other side of the water. However I do admit that there are a few things about East Bog I didn't know about that I do know now.

'The company this week has been stimulating, people as well as birds – here they are given equal status. Work parties are a good idea, long may they continue. Having recovered from the sight of my old frying pan going rusty in the nettles and the chickens drinking out of my old mixing bowl, I must congratulate Sue on the incredible cuisine, the best I remember here. I'm sure everyone else will agree with me. Thanks to everyone – even Paul – for congenial company, stimulating conversation, magpie impersonations etc, etc and thanks especially to Mike and Sue for looking after us and the island so well.'

Huw Morgan, another work party regular and past assistant warden, has the following to say:

'Burdened with the twin responsibilities of improving both legibility and literary merit, I am tempted to write in old Welsh Ogam.

'Work party week – the week that oils the seasonal cogs of Skokholm – has come and gone. Once again the humour, talents, knowledge, calmness, excitability of the merry crew make it as memorable as the previous ones.

'A nod in the direction of bureaucratic necessities meant a new outlook in the cooking facilities. It is quite extraordinary how the hygienic facade of mainland catering can be so quickly transplanted into the homely hearth of Skokholm. It is hard to imagine how it can improve on the already excellent quality of the cuisine.

'On a work party one's stomach becomes most important, it helps give leverage to those difficult rusty screws, which have become embedded and inextricably linked with the wood that holds them. One's stomach lets one know what time of day it is and occasionally what time of night! A work party marches on its stomach.

'Having been part of a few of these momentous occasions, how it heartens and amazes me to see how the disparate members and various tasks marry up in an understated yet understood fashion and get completed in an efficient and "painless" way.

'In the midst of all this work there is still time to do some observing – ring ouzel, black redstart, turnstone, chiffchaff, dunnock, all visitors to the island's resident population – so this is why I sometimes feel like a migrant. I keep coming back and I

123

always will; life makes so much more sense over here somehow – everyone gets on with it. I look forward to the next time – autumn migration perhaps.'

Rod Billen expressed his comments in verse, with a cheeky rhyme, teasing me as leader of a dedicated team, who over the years have made considerable efforts for the wellbeing of the island.

ODE TO OUR ILLUSTRIOUS LEADER
or THE FOREMAN FROM HELL

'I was offered a job on a building site
On Skokholm Island. Great!
I said "Hello" to the foreman, John.
He said "You're three minutes late".

"I've got a cushy number for you,
I think you'll be alright.
Just build three bedrooms over there,
Be teatime tomorrow night".

I said "It's a beautiful morning,
It's great to be alive.
I hope I don't miss Neighbours,
It starts at half past five".

John had an amazing dumper,
It was resting by a gate.
A sticker on the engine said,
Rebuilt in '38.

The Benbow Boys were up from Devon,
They were our carpentry team.
Ray Saunders was their apprentice
On a Youth Employment Scheme.

We'd built the walls by midnight,
A superhuman feat.
Huw Morgan said "When the roof's on
John will let us stop to eat".

Four a.m. at the mixer,
The rain dripped off my specs.
It ran in rivers down my chest,
And eventually down my legs.

Sam said "What a super job,
I really love this place".
I told Sam I didn't agree
And punched him in the face.

124

The wind picked up to Force 8 or 9,
And screaming around our heads.
John said "Get the roof on,
We've got to make some beds".

Renata was there and she's a nurse,
I was pleased but not surprised,
The way John was driving us,
Men were dropping down like flies.

Plastering by candlelight,
Scratch said "We must be nutters".
John said "No time to stand and chat,
Help me with the gutters".

I was totally exhausted,
Collapsed and on all fours;
John said "While you're down there,
You'd better paint the floors".

We've got the building finished,
John gave us a can of beer,
He said "Now you idle buggers,
Do you want a job next year?"

And we said "Yes please"!

ABOVE: Ray Saunders making a 'Skokholm
Slumberland Special'. BELOW: Michael Betts and
the author have a last minute conference.

LEFT: 'Scratch'. RIGHT: The baggage going down to the boat at the end of the week. BELOW: Work party members: seated, Jack Rogers, Stephen Sutcliffe, Ray Saunders, Sam Robins, Jim Poole, Dai Rogers, Peter Hope-Jones, Rosemary Thompson; on ground: author, Theresa Purcell, Graham Thompson.

127

ABOVE: A party in the Common Room. BELOW:
Peter Partington conducting an Art Course.

128

ABOVE: The management 'Inner Cabinet': David
Saunders, Simon Smith (the Skomer Warden),
Stuart Devonald, Jack Donovan, chairman,
Stephen Evans CCW, Graham Thompson, (the
Skokholm Warden). BELOW: Evening feed for the
gulls.

ABOVE: Gull's eye view of the buildings. BELOW:
The sun sets over Grassholm as night claims the
island.

EPILOGUE

Since planning this book Pembrokeshire has suffered the tragedy of a major oil spill, in the form of the *Sea Empress* disaster. Fortunately for Skokholm and Skomer the islands were little affected but, if it had happened a month later and the wind had blown the other way, the sea bird carnage would have been horrendous. Even so the damage done to the local ecosystem and consequent wildlife food supplies is considerable and may not be measured for some time to come.

Looking towards the mainland from Skokholm, because of the tilt of the rock strata between the Deer Park and St Anne's Head, what you are looking at – geologically speaking – is 400 million years of landscape development.

Up to maybe a hundred years ago man's activities on this planet had done little to cause irreparable damage to the environment. To those of us who study the earth's resources and its natural life forms, it is only too distressingly apparent that we are destroying our life systems at a rate that is being compounded with every successive year. Whole species are being decimated at an unprecedented rate, right to the point of extinction. Once gone they will never re-appear and we have to ask ourselves – what God-given right have we to embark on such an orgy of destruction?

It is a sad fact that none of us can put our hand on our hearts and say that we have no part in it all. The oil from the *Sea Empress* could well have been destined for our motor cars, or central heating systems; motorways, urban development, the cutting down of the rain forests, all happen in the name of progress. Never mind that some life forms and in the case of the rain forests, human life forms are destroyed in the process.

Rod Billen, who acted as beachmaster in the oil clean-up operation, told me after a fortnight that he had seen no living thing: no crab, shrimp, jellyfish – nothing, the whole shoreline was a stinking desert.

I have a favourite spot on Spy Rock where I can sit in solitude with the infinity of space above and the limitless ocean at my feet. I cannot help but think what an insignificant speck I am, compared with the vastness all around me and how transient I am in the world's development. But never before in the whole of time has a single individual, exactly the same as me, possessed the power to blow everything to smithereens.

131

So I ask myself the question, is it part of the scheme of things that mankind should exploit the resources given him, which if continued at the present rate must soon turn the globe into a desert? Or are we a maverick species of life that has somehow got out of control?

Those of us who visit Skokholm and the ever fewer solitary places, realise how life was meant to be lived. We try to exert our influence and make people aware of the dangers to the world's lifeforce. Few listen and even fewer are prepared to act.

On a more positive note there is a slowly emerging groundswell of opinion, not all of them cranks, recognising the dangers facing this planet. Whether it will become strong enough to influence those controlling the areas that matter, before the desert arrives on our doorsteps, is a question that is very much in the balance.

We should never forget that the many species of life inhabiting the world are interdependent on each other. The human race is also a form of wildlife.

List of Stockholm Wardens.

1933-1939	R. M. Lockley in full time residence. John Buxton for the summer of 1939, when the island was evacuated.
1946	John Fursdon
1946-1954	Peter Conder/Peter Davis
1954-1956	Peter Davis
1957	George Edwards
1958-1959	Kate Barham
1961-1962	Don Glanville
1963-1965	Mike Harris
1966-1969	Chris Britton
1970-1971	Barry Chambers
1972	John Davis
1973-1976	Mike Brook
1977-1978	Ray Lawman
1979-1980	Steve Warman
1981-1984	Graham Gynn
1985-1986	Rob Wolstenholme
1987-1995	Michael Betts
1996-	Graham Thompson

Index

ENDPAPERS: Map of Skokholm.

134

SUBSCRIBERS

Presentation Copies

1 R. M. Lockley
2 Skokholm Library
3 Skomer Library
4 Peter Partington
5 Stephen Sutcliffe

6 John & Helen Lewis
7 Clive & Carolyn Birch
8 Mick & Anne Brown
9 Sam Robins
10 Eve Hobill
11 Elizabath Pengelly
12 Rod Billen
13 Huw Morgan
14 Graham & Liz Gynn
15 Patricia Johnstone
16 Sally Franklin
17 Clive Billen
18 Ted Billen
19 Mrs S. Tippett
20-21 Mrs A. Ballard
22 Peter Garrod
23 John Applin
24 Mrs Yvonne Evans
25 Chrisopher & Carys Bell
26 Arthur & Ethel Lambert
27 Diane Atkins
28 M. Hall
29 David Stanbury MBE
30 Tony Soper
31 R. Couchman
32 John Parker
33 Norman, Virginia & Matthew Hawkins
34 Russ Spenceley
35 Timothy Scott
36 Michael J. Wilson
37 A.L. Leigh
38 Ann Benn
39 John Blake
40 Ted & Molly Elliott
41 Jan Schubert
42 John Bell
43 Anne M. McCall
44 David, Sharon & John Jr Lewis
45 C.G. & E.A. Humphris
46 Roger Gershon
47 Glynis Dovey
48 Greg Morgan
49 Jean Lawman

50 Tony Carey
51 Bill Hynes
52 C.F. Samuelson
53 A.B. Kehoe
54 David Howells
55 David A.C. Jones
56 Ron & Sheila Hanley
57 R. Padmore
58 Mr & Mrs J.A. & G.M. King
59 David A. Quinn
60 Miss Phylis Jackson
61 Mrs F.C. Felton
62 Lyndon Whyatt
63 D.W. Reay
64 Mike Lacey
65 D. & P.A. Cox
66 R.J. Hayward
67 Cecilly Haussmann
68 Les Borg
69 John A. Jones
70 Miss B.E.H. Bell
71 Helen Lewis
72 Heidi Lewis
73-74 Graham Thompson
75 C. Wilkinson
76 R.A. Phelps
77 Stephen Halton
78 M. Overton
79 Diana Bradley
80 Alan George
81 T.A. Theobald
82 David R.G. Hill
83 Colin Selwood
84 Anne Kehoe
85 Keith & Suzie Usher
86 D.C. May
87 R.J. Keene
88 Ian Tugwell
89 Barry Bealey
90 A.R. Wynde
91 Huw Morgan
92 Stewart Rogers
93 David Rogers
94 Jack & Audrey Rogers

95 Margaret R. Lee
96 Jill Saint
97 Keith Rowley
98 M.H. Oughton
99 Jill Harrison
100 Rex Haggett
101 B.T. Parkes
102 Claire J. Tyres
103 Kagoshima Immaculate Heart College Library
104 Philip Blatcher
105 Jean Elkins
106 Richard Boyd
107 Jean Harborne
108 Peter & Kathleen Sheldon
109 Gladys M. Reynolds
110 C. Aston
111 C.F. Dibble
112 C.T. Dowse
113 Mel Veal
114 David J. Rice
115 M.B. Williams
116 Ralph & Barbara Tomlinson
117 Ian D.C. Shephard
118 Dave Reynolds
119 Les Tollitt
120 Brian Tollitt
121 Dr Timothy Bagenal
122 Nicholas Goozee
123 E.A. Bourn
124 R.P. Fuller
125 Patricia Atkins
126 R.F. Arnold
127 Maurice Morgan
128 Mrs G.J.Wallis
129 Phil Berry
130 Russell Wood
131 Patricia Harrison
132 Mrs B.J. Day-Squire
133 Hazel Blewett
134 Terry Henshaw
135 H.J. Bell
136 Peter Hirst
137 Mary & Gordon Ayres
138 David A. Jones

The last bird – approximately 40,000 shearwaters
nest on Skokholm.

136

SKOKHOLM ISLAND

li

north gul(

mad bay
point

twinlet bay

no
po

purple
cove

mad bay

western plain

the b

wallsend
bay

tabernacle
rock

south-
pond

wildgoose
bay

blulls

sugar loaf

winter
pond

the quarry

L.H.

the dip

0   100 m   50